GODS IN STRANGE PLACES

The Untold Story of the Maya

GLEN E. FULLER

c.1

By the same author

THE MAYA — A Legacy in Stone © 1980

Printed in the United States of America
Salt Lake City, Utah

TOPICS

ACKNOWLEDGMENTS

It is customary procedure to preface a semitechnical book by extending credit to the many contributors who assisted in bringing forth the literary child of their endeavors. After having written and arranged this work, I find it to be somewhat unusual in that it has resulted from the efforts of a very few individuals.

For more than 150 years a great number of scholars, explorers and adventurers have poured forth many volumes on the subject of the Maya. A great deal of accumulated information appears to be, and has been accepted by me as, authentic, and much of what has been handed down constitutes foundational material for this book. However, it is my considered opinion that long-held assumptions involving several areas of Maya activity relating to the manner in which their great stone edifices were constructed — and which are of critical importance in understanding their civilization — have been based upon unsupportable and faulty premises. Believing that an in-depth examination should be made of the stone-work of the Maya, since it represents most of the legacy which they have handed down, this work enters uncharted waters in an effort to expose and correct some long accepted and inaccurate beliefs which for too long have been taken for granted.

The new and different concepts advanced in this work have required a great deal of soul searching and study on my part and, quite frankly, the journey through the following pages has sometimes been rather lonely. There has been no staff of collaborators and co-workers to lean upon; no grant from any private or public source has financed any part of this effort; and, except for isolated excerpts gleaned from research as noted in the text, there is no bibliography to draw upon in the area where I have departed from the well-traveled route. Even among the ruins, the door is now closed to any intensive investigation, since the respective governments of Mexico, Guatemala and Honduras have given national park status to their major ruins so as to preserve national treasures. Merely placing one's foot on a stone relic will bring forth an armed guard who will advise that one must not touch. Nevertheless, this book had to be written — it is long overdue.

A substantial amount of input has been contributed by my long-time law and business associate, Jack R. Decker, who accompanied me on three of my five excursions into the Yucatan Peninsula. His incisive and analytical mind provided a testing arena as we spent many days and nights exploring and discussing our findings. His presence in the jungle was a constant source of support; moreover, his many hours of research into long-forgotten and remote publications have made possible a logical presentation of this subject.

It is no easy task to ferret out those features of Maya life which contributed most to the rise and eventual fall of that splendid civilization in the jungles of Mesoamerica; it is an even greater challenge to bring many critical elements into focus so as to provide a plausible presentation that will make sense to the avid reader. In this respect, due credit must be given to Mary McHenry, who has been my secretary for over 20 years and whose loyal and tireless efforts, support and assistance have made it possible to put the message of this work into print.

Throughout the six-year life of this project, I have been most fortunate in having the support and assistance of my wife, Connie, whose contributions have been extended in many direct and indirect ways that cannot be counted and which, in cumulative effect, have permitted me to concentrate on the task at hand. Likewise, my son, Kim G. Fuller, has spent much of his working life in our family stone quarry in northern Utah, and in preparing this work he has produced or assisted in the presentation of several of the illustrative sketches. Last, but by no means least, the artistry of Jan Burke, as expressed in her superb watercolor painting introducing the Chapter *"An Era of New Technology"* and several provocative, stylized sketches located in the text and on the cover of this book, makes a substantial contribution to the presentation of our story.

To this small group I extend my sincere appreciation.

GEF

THE AUTHOR

Mr. Fuller has spent a lifetime deeply involved in various real property activities. Reared on a crop and livestock farm in northern Utah, he has owned and operated agricultural lands for many years.

He received his B.S. degree in Economics from Utah State University in 1942. Subsequently, as a Newell Scholar, he attended Stanford University where he received his Juris Dr. degree in 1947. He is admitted to practice law in and has appeared before the state courts of Utah and California, and he has handled major cases before the U.S. Tax Court, the U.S. Claims Court, the U.S. Tenth Circuit Court of Appeals and the U.S. Supreme Court.

Since 1948, he has been a practicing trial lawyer and real property appraiser, specializing in residential, commercial, industrial, recreational and mineral properties (including building stone deposits) in condemnation and eminent domain litigation on behalf of property owners. During that time he has actually tried or settled nearly 500 litigated cases.

In 1954 he discovered and filed federal mining claims on turquoise - colored quartzite stone deposits in the Raft River Mountains of northern Utah. As co-owner and manager of Fuller Quarries, he has been active in a family business of quarrying and distributing "Turquoise" stone products throughout the United States and into Canada. This operation has continued without interruption for 30 years as a successful adjunct to his law practice.

Fuller Quarries and its predecessor company have been long-time members of the international Building Stone Institute, a trade association representing stone quarriers and all other segments of the stone industry. Mr Fuller is a past president of that organization and was one of its directors for many years.

In 1960, he was appointed general counsel and a director of Portland Cement Company of Utah, a producer of Portland cement utilizing limestone and other cement-making materials from quarries which it owned and worked. In 1979, Lone Star Industries, Inc., the largest cement producer in the United States, acquired full ownership of Portland Cement Company of Utah, and he has been retained by Lone Star as a director and as general counsel for its Utah operations.

Mr. Fuller is also the founder and president of The Fuller Foundation.

TEMPLE OF THE INSCRIPTIONS AT PALENQUE

The Maya constructed some temple pyramids as sepulchral monuments in the manner of the Egyptians. The Funerary Crypt of Pacal was enclosed within and at the bottom of the structure, accessible from an interior stairway which was concealed beneath a large stone slab located on the temple floor at the top of the Pyramid.

INTRODUCTION

During the past 3,500 years or more, according to archaeologists, a people now known as the Maya developed a civilization in those portions of Central America which include Guatemala, Belize (formerly British Honduras), the western portion of San Salvador and Honduras, and the Chiapas and Yucatan Peninsula portions of Mexico. This land comprises a substantial portion of what has also been designated as Mesoamerica. One of the most striking features of the entire area is its extensive, rugged terrain, varying from vast expanses of rough, serrated jungle to volcanic peaks towering 14,000 feet into the sky. Mountains, canyons, ravines and broken landscapes are commonplace. Tillable land is usually found in small, scattered patches and, even then, its use is often limited by a combination of adverse factors.

Most Stone Age civilizations have left us with no more than a limited number of simple structures, or a few paintings or artifacts, to record their existence. The Maya, on the other hand, ventured into an extremely harsh and forbidding jungle domain, nearly devoid of natural resources and presenting obstacles to life at every turn, and proceeded to construct great numbers of imposing stone monuments. Everyone visiting this land today, whether student, professional or tourist, is thrilled and awed at the marvels performed by its ancient inhabitants. How and why they were able to perform such feats have completely baffled all who have probed for answers in the silence of that vast expanse of jungle spread across the Yucatan Peninsula.

The history of the Maya as they populated this land would have been a rather routine occurrence common to many other peoples during the advance of civilization, except for a great burst of building activity and a development of the arts which reached its zenith and culminated during what is known as the Late Classic period — approximately 600 to 900 A.D. Among other achievements of that time, the Maya created and built most of their extensive ceremonial complexes of stone, consisting of pyramid temples, palaces and other structures. In fact, were it not for the legacy in stone which has survived in the form of great ruins across the land, it is unlikely that history would have devoted more than a few pages to their existence.

Archaeologists have found it convenient to segregate Maya country into two rather distinct physical segments: the "highlands" and the "lowlands." The highlands lie at an elevation exceeding approximately 1,000 feet above sea level; the lowlands are located mostly below the 1,000 foot elevation level and northerly of the edge of the mountainous spine of Central America in the region commonly known as the Yucatan Peninsula. The Peninsula embraces the Petén (northern) portion of Guatemala; Belize; and the States of Campeche, Yucatan, Quintana Roo, and portions of Chiapas and Tabasco, in Mexico. It is approximately 200 miles wide and spreads out across the lowlands in a northerly direction for about 300 miles.

The Yucatan Peninsula is a great limestone shelf which has arisen over a great period of time from the bed of an ancient sea. Although appearing to be level and flat from the air, the irregular terrain is hid-

Modern Maya in the countryside live in huts having dirt floors, pole walls and thatched roofs. The homes of their ancestors were built in the same manner.

den in a sea of greenery. Overlaying the land is an almost continuous jungle, ranging from tropical growth with trees exceeding 100 feet in height in the Petén portion of Guatemala to a tough, thorny cover of trees and vines ranging from 15 to 40 feet in height in the northern portion of the Peninsula. The inland area has been characterized as being one, great "living rock," and there are only limited pockets of very shallow soil susceptible to being farmed.

Rains begin in May and usually end in early November (except in Belize, east of the Maya Mountains), but unusually long dry periods sometimes occur during the rainy season. The southern portion of the Peninsula will average about 80 inches of rainfall a year; the northern portion receives about half that amount. During the hot dry season from November through April there are often dry spells when no rain

THE INLAND
YUCATAN PENINSULA
(shaded)

Dzibilchaltún
Merida
CHICHÉN ITZÁ
Cancún
Cobá
Mayapán
UXMAL
Kabáh
Tulum
Sayil
Cozumel
Labná

GULF OF
MEXICO

MEXICO

Becan
Chetumal
Kohunlich

PALENQUE
El Mirador
Uaxactún
CARIBBEAN
SEA
TIKAL
MEXICO
BELIZE
Yaxchilán
Bonampak
Lake Petén

GUATEMALA

Quiriguá

COPÁN

Guatemala City
HONDURAS

PACIFIC
OCEAN
EL
SALVADOR

NORTH

4

will fall for months at a time, although moist air from the seacoast does tend to maintain a relatively high level of humidity year-round. Worse still, rainfall quickly permeates the underlying limestone, leaving most of the inland Peninsula without springs, rivers or lakes. Except for the Lake Petén area of Guatemala and for scattered *cenotes* (breaks in the limestone crust which open up so as to allow access to the underground water table), there are few locations where sufficient domestic water can be found to support human settlements.

The *inland* Yucatan Peninsula will be specifically and repeatedly segregated for discussion in this work; for most purposes, it will relate to the geographic portion which lies inland a distance of 30 miles (approximately 50 kilometers) from, and parallel to, the sea which surrounds it on the east, north and west. The present population of the inland area is meager and widely dispersed.

Curiously, it was in the harsh and forbidding environment of the inland Yucatan Peninsula that the Maya civilization flourished and withered. What the Maya accomplished in the highland country, except for a few isolated instances, is of little concern to us; what captures the imagination are the magnificent, abandoned ceremonial centers whose paradoxical presence in desolate locations in the brooding silence of the lowland jungle conjure up mysteries for which there have been few clues and no acceptable answers.

Without any kind of wheeled contrivance and lacking any beasts of burden, the Maya carried every building stone from its quarry source to the final structure by utilizing human energy, usually assisted by the tumpline with a band across the forehead to help support the loads carried on their backs. Further, unlike the Egyptians, Greeks or Romans, the Maya quarried, shaped and dressed their stones without the benefit of metal tools   a task seemingly impossible for any Stone Age people to accomplish.

As mentioned, the Yucatan Peninsula is a great limestone platform pushed up from the sea. And since references to limestone will be made throughout this book, a few words about this material are appropriate. Limestone is a mineral substance having many uses, its chemical composition being primarily calcium carbonate ($CaCO_3$). As is the case with most minerals, nature deposits its treasures in strange places and in numerous combinations; therefore, it is not at all uncommon to find different kinds of limestone, with varying chemical and physical ingredients and characteristics, in many places.

The limestone of the Yucatan Peninsula is essentially of organic origin; that is to say, its composition has resulted from accretions of small sea animals whose remains were deposited on the watery floor of an ancient sea. Accordingly, most of that limestone contains very little or no inorganic, or earthy, materials, such as sand or gravel derived from quartzitic, igneous or granite rocks.

A critical consideration when dealing with the workability of stone, particularly when approached with the knowledge that the subject people had no metal tools, is that of its relative hardness. The modern measure of grading minerals for hardness is the Moh rating scale, which establishes a point range extending downward from 10.0. A diamond is rated at 10.0; other precious stones, such as emeralds and rubies, run in the 8.0 to 9.0 range. Hard quartzites range between 5.5 and 7.0; granites generally are in the 5.0 to 6.0 range; and marbles are usually 4.0 to 5.0 in hardness. Limestones, which exhibit wide variations from deposit to deposit, vary from approximately 2.0 to 3.5 in hardness.

I visited the Yucatan ruins at Chich'en Itz'a and Uxmal in 1967 and, after examining the limestone used by the Maya on those structures, came away with the firm opinion that much of that stone — some of which was yellowish-orange and glassy in appearance — had a hardness rating of approximately 3.5. But of most concern, after looking at structures having smooth-faced and well-shaped building blocks, I arrived at a conclusion which once again brought me back to Maya country in January, 1979:

> The Maya absolutely could not have quarried, faced and shaped the hundreds of thousands of building blocks used on their structures with simple stone tools.

Fortified with more than 25 years of background experience in laying and quarrying limestone and quartzite stone, a layman's exposure to geology gleaned from first-hand field work with some of the best experts in the United States, and being conversant with the production of cement from limestone sources, I eagerly, but with some hesitation, approached the problems with which I was confronted. Could it just be possible that a clue to some of the mysteries surrounding the Maya might be found by investigating such a simple and mundane subject as the stone from which they constructed their great works?

For 150 years almost everyone who has written about the Maya has asserted that there was (and, by simple logic, there still should be — but, unfortunately, isn't) an inexhaustible supply of limestone on the Yucatan Peninsula which could be easily quarried and cut with flint or other stone tools. As a consequence of such largess and by utilizing hordes of workmen, as the argument proceeds, it was possible to take blocks of rough stone and peck smooth faces and trim and cut square and rectangular shapes on them so as to produce facing blocks for their structures. Numerous articles can be found explaining in a general way how the job was done, usually backing away from detailed illustrations and furnishing, instead, broad, generalized explanations; yet, I have been unable to find a single instance where an advocate of any theory has taken a hard limestone rock in hand and proceeded to "peck" a smooth, rectangular face on an otherwise rough and irregular stone surface. Nor, for that matter, has anyone explained how a block of stone could be removed from a large, solid mass by chipping and chiseling it away, using only flint or other stone tools.

Despite extensive investigations at numerous sites, there has been a conspicuous absence of any finds or caches of stone tools which might have been used for quarrying, cutting, chiseling or pecking purposes. There have been two isolated finds of "masonry tool kits" containing objects used for plastering and abrading purposes, but practically nothing has been found in the line of stone-cutting tools.

The great ceremonial centers of the Maya have given rise to a host of intriguing mysteries: Why were their great "cities" built in such unlikely locations; how many workmen were required in their construction; how many people did they serve; why were they all abandoned to the jungle by 900 A.D.; and where did the "millions of people" inhabiting those "cities" go? To compound the problem, I was searching for the answer to the even greater mystery of how the Maya were able to build their ceremonial centers in the first instance — an impossible task by all standards I could apply.

Perhaps if I could solve the seldom-approached and most-basic problem, as I perceived it, it might be possible to shed some light on the other long-standing mysteries of the Maya. That such an investigation had merit was supported by the fact that, except for occasional supporting lintel beams of sapodilla or other hardwood above the entryways to the rooms of some of their structures, and round poles which often spanned room vaults above head height, Maya construction consisted 100% of stone.

In 1932, J. Eric Thompson noted in a published article that there were widely divergent architectural styles among the various ceremonial centers at different locations on the Peninsula, and he suggested that it ". . . would be interesting for a geologist to make a survey of the structural possibilities of the limestone encountered in different parts of the Maya area."

To my knowledge, no geologist or any other qualified expert has made such a study nor, for that matter, would such a study likely provide the answers we are seeking. Further, as will be revealed as our story unfolds, the lack of direct evidence would most likely preclude a geologist from finding the necessary clues. Nevertheless, much wasted effort might have been avoided over the past 50 years if Thompson's suggestion had been taken seriously.

. . . .

When Jack Decker and I flew my single-engine Cessna 182 plane across the border of northern Mexico on January 20, 1979, little did we realize where our journey would ultimately take us. Admittedly, I was looking for the answer to a precise question, but I was a bit too naive at the time to realize that the answer might take me far afield of my original objective.

We both felt that a flying inspection of Mesoamerica might give a different perspective to an understanding of Maya stone construction, particularly since it would provide an "overview" which might make it easier to make comparisons of the various ruins we planned to visit. A few writers had advanced the proposition, in which I concurred, that the collapse of Maya civilization was related to problems or events common to the entire area, and it was my purpose to search for conditions or clues which might provide common denominators in approaching the subject.

It is difficult to comprehend the extent and magnitude of the Yucatan Peninsula until one observes it from a low-flying plane. The Petén jungle portion which lies in Guatemala is a vast region with extremely limited pockets of human habitation. Roads of any kind are few and far between. Spreading across the vast, endless expanse of irregular terrain and smothering the entire Peninsula is the jungle — brooding, dark, and everywhere preserving its secrets in an entangling growth.

The scene beneath our wings indicated a combination of physical conditions which certainly would not appear conducive to supporting or encouraging human settlements. We were given to understand that in recent years Guatemala had encouraged its people to settle in the area and offered subsidies to encourage its development, but as soon as possible the settlers returned to Guatemala City and its pleasant climate.

This story is about stone, a somewhat more sophisticated word than "rock," and at times the two words might be used interchangeably. Although one might expect the subject to be dull, it is highly interesting, especially if we stop to realize that stone was an object near and dear to Stone Age peoples. In plain language and by using illustrations, we will analyze the stone-quarrying and construction methods of the greatest Stone Age builders who ever roamed the earth.

Numerous references will be made throughout this book to a particular "stone deposit" located at a so-called ceremonial center, the quoted words being used collectively to refer to all of the stone available at that site. Occasionally, however, the plural words "stone deposits" will be used to refer to physically separated areas or portions of a larger over-all stone deposit. For example, the total "stone deposit" at Chichén Itzá (as well as each respective "stone deposit" at Uxmal, Tikal or Palenque) covered a land area of over a mile in extent, and included within that stone deposit would have been several smaller stone deposits.

This book follows my 1980 abbreviated treatise *The Maya — A Legacy in Stone*, and it will be my purpose to reveal many of the hows, whys and wheres of Maya stone-work. In the process we may be so fortunate as to find clues to some of the great mysteries of the Maya which have remained unsolved for nearly 500 years since the Spaniards arrived in the New World and, in particular, during the last 150 years of intensive study by many scholars.

Throughout this book several key points will be periodically repeated; at other times, in order to impress a given point, a statement or illustration will be set forth in two or more different ways. The repetition may be somewhat redundant, but it must be appreciated that this book is the result of five extensive trips into Maya country covering the same ground, so to speak, with each trip supplying bits and pieces of significant information necessary to complete the framework of this story.

The basic premises set forth in this work break completely new ground in understanding some of the mysteries of the Maya, and so it is necessary to return to them again and again as the puzzle falls into place. The story is being related in the sequence that it actually developed in my mind as I traveled through the land of the Maya, and I must confess that my mental processes work best when I can form a clear, mental image or physically look at and feel the object of my investigation. In short, I learn best by actual experience, and though the method might be slow and repetitious, such has been the lifelong process by which these pages have come into being. And if, as we proceed, I might adopt a lawyer's writing style and occasionally revert to legalese, I hope to be excused.

We will be concerned primarily with the great (and partially restored) Yucatan Peninsula ceremonial centers of Tikal, Chich'en Itz'a, Uxmal and Palenque, as well as Cop'an in Honduras. Some of those centers may have had beginnings pre-dating the Christian era, and occupancy and some stone construction may have been present in a somewhat continuous pattern during subsequent centuries, but that story is the special province of the archaeologists. Our concern will be directed primarily to the period of time between 600 and 900 A.D., more commonly known as the Late Classic era, when the great majority of the existing stone structures were built on those sites. It was the Golden Age of the Maya.

The many visitors, students and others interested in the Maya and their imposing structures, including many who have spent years in Maya country digging in the ruins and risking their health and lives in search of answers to the mysteries of that people, are entitled to a new and practical base of knowledge from which their future efforts will be productive and satisfying. It is the purpose of this book to supply that foundation and to remove much of the fog which has heretofore enshrouded Maya history.

As our story unfolds and the overall picture of the Maya and their stone structures comes into focus, it will be possible to better assess the sobering message left by that gifted people for all nations on earth.

TIKAL

THE INLAND
YUCATAN PENINSULA
(shaded)

- Dzibilchaltún
★ Merida   CHICHÉN ITZÁ   • Cancún
                    • Cobá
        • Mayapán
UXMAL •   Tulum •
    • Kabáh   Cozumel
    • Sayil
        • Labná

GULF OF
MEXICO

MEXICO

    Becan •
            Chetumal
        Kohunlich •

★
Villahermosa

PALENQUE •   El Mirador •
            Uaxactún •
            TIKAL •   CARIBBEAN
                            SEA
                    BELIZE

MEXICO
        Yaxchilán • Lake Petén
        Bonampak

    GUATEMALA

            Quiriguá •

    Guatemala City
        ★   • COPÁN

                    HONDURAS
PACIFIC
OCEAN
            EL
            SALVADOR

↑

NORTH

**The Great Plaza, with the Central Acropolis in the background,
was the heart of Late Classic Tikal.**

TIKAL

We were standing among a group of tourists in the Great Plaza of Tikal. Here, in the Petén jungle of Northern Guatemala on the leveled tops of numerous high ridges, there can be found within a radius of less than a mile several other major plazas with their complexes of pyramids and surrounding structures. Jungle trees rise on all sides to a height of as much as 150 feet, exceeded only by the roof combs of pyramid temples rising above the jungle growth.

We had recently arrived at the Tikal Park headquarters from Flores, a settlement on Lake Petén some 40 miles farther south, and after a short stop we boarded a local minibus and commenced a steep ascent to the Great Plaza. The abrupt elevation change of some 200 feet in less than a half-mile was something unexpected since my sources of information clearly sta ted that Tikal was located in a lowland jungle. Jungle it is; lowland it is not, except in the context of being in the broad geographic area so-defined. A check of my topographic map revealed the Great Plaza to be approximately 820 feet above sea level. This seems a bit unusual because at that altitude, on the very crown of a group of ridges, Tikal is on one of the highest points in the Guatemalan and Mexican portions of the Yucatan Peninsula.

A young English-speaking guide, recently graduated from a British school in nearby Belize, was explaining the features of the spectacle to the group. His routine remarks were rehearsed and adapted to the typical questions of awe-struck tourists. My extensive experience during many years as a stone quarrier prompted me to explore a bit deeper into the situation, and so I ventured an inquiry.

"Why did the Maya build on this, the highest place in the jungle?" I asked.

"Because there were deposits of flint for carving stone in the vicinity, and here, on this great acropolis, the Maya could view their world and live safely above the unhealthy swamps," he answered.

"And where were the quarries located from which they secured the stone for these massive structures?"

He shrugged, obviously annoyed that an overly inquisitive tourist would bother him with such mundane trifles, and casually pointed to the deep ravines beyond and below the floor of the plaza. Rather interesting, I mused, since everyone I had read on the the subject advanced the same explanation.

But why, I pondered, would a community choose to live in such a desolate area where the steep terrain was neither conducive to an urban settlement nor compatible with agricultural pursuits? The general locality depended on large, open cisterns or reservoirs for water, there being no stream sources in the area, and deep wells which had been drilled in modern times produced only dry holes. The only pockets of present-day population in a radius of 40 air miles are in the vicinity of

Lake Petén and along the western border of Belize.

Any view across the jungle from the various plazas of Tikal always would have been hidden by jungle trees, except from the tops of the highest pyramids, and the scene presented by the monotonous expanse of jungle would not have made that effort worthwhile. It struck me as incomprehensible that any people would have undertaken the task of leveling the tops of steep ridges without machines or metal tools, then dropping below into the deep, surrounding ravines to quarry building stones, and then packing them uphill to the leveled mound and upwards another 150 to 200 feet to the tops of their pyramids. Allowing for a tolerable angle of climb, simple logistics would indicate the average distance of travel for every stone carried by human labor would have been about 500 feet, with the vertical rise constituting nearly one-half of the total distance.

Nor did the contours of the observable ravines or the lines on the topographic map give the slightest indication that the massive quantities of stone in the pyramids and buildings around the Great Plaza and the other complexes of ruins could have come from ravines below the plaza. My background experience told me that quarries and ravines usually go hand-in-hand with waste dumps, of which I could find none, and I had yet to see any construction operation where large quantities of stone were manually hauled uphill from a nearby quarry to build structures of any kind.

My sole purpose in coming to the Yucatan Peninsula in January and February of 1979 was to determine exactly how the Maya were able to make smooth-faced limestone building blocks with only stone tools at their disposal. Some twelve years earlier I had examined the pyramids and buildings at Chichén Itza, and I came away firmly convinced that the task was impossible. And yet, ironically, I was standing in the midst of another group of smooth, symmetrically shaped stone structures built by a Stone Age civilization.

We had flown to Oaxaca, Mexico, and from there we visited nearby Monte Albán with its plazas and low pyramids built of a soft, inorganic rock, composed in large measure of volcanic substances and which in appearance looked partly like argillite and partly like sand-

The hulking form of Pyramid V (unrestored) faces north across the Great Plaza. It is 190 feet high.

stone. The material was easily dislodged from the ridgetop where it was found and it required little or no shaping or trimming. We also traveled about 20 miles beyond Oaxaca to the ruins at Mitla where a relatively soft volcanic-type stone had been worked into mosaic patterns and building blocks. None of the structures at either of those ruins gave me any concern, nor did those ruins furnish any assistance in solving the problem which again confronted me at Tikal, because the materials being worked at the two sites near Oaxaca did not require the use of any tools other than harder stones.

The same baffling problem encountered at Chichén Itzá was present at every hand among the ruins at Tikal. The utter frustration of knowing that the smooth-faced limestone blocks on those structures absolutely could not have been made by stone tools, such as flint or

Pyramid II (called the Temple of the Masks) is located at the west end of the Great Plaza.

rocks even harder than limestone, was only surpassed by staring at the proof and wondering how it was done. It was this challenge that had brought me back to the Yucatan Peninsula.

Every writer who has approached the subject of Maya stone-work has gone along with the widely held belief that great numbers of workmen were utilized in quarrying and shaping the stones found on the outer facings of the numerous pyramids and palaces. Whenever any attempt has been made to detail the process involved, the explanation usually given has been that each separate block of stone was individually chiseled and cut by one or two workmen from a solid mass of limestone. Using only stone tools, the workmen would approach a wall of stone and then chip and cut away the bottom, top and both sides of the intended stone from the solid rock outcropping. The workmen would peck and chip away on the front side of the stone until it had a

17

smooth face and a square or rectangular shape, thus enabling it to be used as a facing block on a pyramid or building. After preparing the face of the stone and cutting away the four sides, the object would then be protruding from the solid mass of rock, and the workmen would then chisel around behind the other five sides of the stone they had been working on or, by a combination of chiseling and breaking, it finally would be dislodged from the larger mass of which it was once a part. Illustrations of the foregoing process can also be found in various museum sketches.

If we stop for a moment and analyze the foregoing procedure, it will be apparent that there are some very real problems in making a stone block by that means. Aside from the conclusion I had reached years ago that the job could not be accomplished with stone tools due to the hardness of the limestone the Maya were working with, it can be seen that cutting and chipping would have required striking blows against the stone at an angle, making it very difficult to produce a smooth face or, for that matter, a level face. Also, in order to cut beneath the intended stone, as well as around the sides, the workmen would have had to chip and cut away a substantial portion of the larger mass of stone so as to create a working area beneath, and at least on one side of, the desired object. Working in such close quarters would have limited most of the activity to that of a single workman, and unless he did much of the chipping and chiseling in the awkward position of lying on his back or side, it would have been necessary to undercut the stone rather substantially so that much of the chipping and chiseling could have been done in a kneeling position. It takes little imagination to visualize that the procedure just outlined would have produced chips and very small chunks of stone as waste material which in total amount would have weighed far more than the stone which finally emerged.

When one views the problems of the method I have just explained, there can be little wonder why the belief has developed that the job required vast amounts of labor. On the other hand, as a stone quarrier, it appeared equally unbelievable to me that any people on the face of the earth could ever have been committed to such drudgery.

I took my tape measure and measured various facing stones on the pyramids and buildings and came up with a random variety of measurements: 5 ½ . 6, 13, 18, 19, 24 and 25 inches. One would think that if stones were created by the method previously outlined, there surely would have been some standardized unit of measurement adopted, but every effort to find some such standard proved fruitless.

If the Maya had cut and chipped each individual building stone from a large, solidified mass, we must conclude that such controlled activity and the corresponding expenditure of time and effort would have resulted in very few reject-type stones. In this area, however, we find a contradictory situation in that the cores of the large pyramids and other structures contain a volume of rough, shapeless stones which in number far exceed the better stones used for wall facings. Actually, a visual examination of those stones clearly reveals that they were not individually cut and chiseled from a larger stone mass.

A basic understanding of the methods used in quarrying solid stone deposits will establish the following criteria:

(1) A solid stone mass with a hardness *not exceeding approximately 2.5 Moh,* such as some sandstone deposits, conceivably could be penetrated to limited depths to create small tunnels or caves by the expenditure of great effort and with the aid of considerably harder stone objects, but this effect would be accomplished more likely by pounding or abrading, rather than chipping and cutting; in any event, the production of even a few building blocks by this primitive method would be practically impossible.

(2) To reduce a large, solid mass of stone to smaller sizes involves a separation process whereby the mass can be "attacked" and, broadly speaking, "leveraged," causing manageable portions to be separated therefrom, illustrated by (a) slicing through the deposit at spaced distances with wire saws (as is done in the famous marble deposits of Cararra, Italy), or (b) by drilling into the mass at carefully selected spots — usually along a ledge face — so that an explosive charge will break away numerous portions for further crushing or breaking, or (c) by drilling or chiseling a series of holes in a

straight line along the top surface of an exposed stone deposit at designated intervals so that wood or metal wedges can be driven into the holes, thereby breaking loose large blocks of stone (as was done by the Egyptians in quarrying their famous obelisks) — methods utilizing metal tools and equipment unavailable to Stone Age workers.

(3) Some large stone masses can be reduced to smaller sizes by prying loose individual chunks of stone along cracks caused by natural earth forces or seam lines which were created when the stone mass was formed in the distant past — another and simpler application of "leveraging."

The Maya, having no metal tools, could only utilize stone deposits where either or both of the two conditions in the preceding sub-paragraph (3) were in existence. As a practical matter, most large stone masses having vertical-type natural-pressure breaks (i.e., cracks) can only be ripped apart by heavy modern-day equipment, such as crawler tractors with dozer blades or ripper-type attachments, unless, of course, nature has done the job by natural means so as to create piles of broken rubble stone, as are sometimes found in stone "slides," but these are not usually associated with limestone deposits.

In view of the foregoing analysis, the quarrying options available to the Stone Age Maya were extremely limited.

On considering Tikal's elevated and remote location, coupled with the obvious problems of pursuing agriculture in such a rugged terrain, the question presents itself as to why the Maya ever chose to build there. The theory has been advanced that it was an important trade center, and that certainly may have been a factor justifying its existence. But that factor must be considered in the context of other nearby Maya settlements which were also found in somewhat less-than-desirable locations, such as Uaxactún and El Mirador. When Victor W. von Hagen wrote *World of the Maya*, he visited the ruins of Uaxactún, situated a few miles north of Tikal, and observed that it was located ". . .where one might believe that men with a wide choice would never found a city, in the low, humid jungle-bound El Petén." The inquiry didn't enter my mind at that time, but did the founders of

Tikal is noted for its many stelae and altars.

Tikal and Uaxactún actually have a wide choice of sites for those cities? Or, for that matter, were those great ruins the remains of real "cities," according to modern definitions?

For sheer size the numerous plazas and the volume of pyramids and other structures at Tikal must give it the distinction of being the largest ceremonial complex ever built by the Maya. If a larger ceremonial complex exists, such as El Mirador lying to the northwest near the boundary of Guatemala, it will require years of excavation and restoration to support any challenge to supremacy.

A majority of the plazas and their structures at Tikal can be found within a radius of one mile from the Great Plaza, with plaza elevations ranging from 750 to 850 feet above sea level. As indicated, there are no points in the terrain immediately surrounding Tikal higher than the

The North Acropolis, contiguous to the Great Plaza, reveals 1,000 years of building activity. Successive stages of construction exist, with each group of structures having been erected over earlier buildings which were demolished.

plazas where the structures occur, and from those heights the ravines fall away on all sides into the jungle, thus indicating that at some time in the distant past the forces of nature exerted an extraordinary effort to push this unique spot to a higher elevation than most other areas of the Yucatan Peninsula.

Archaeologists tell us that Tikal was probably inhabited by 500 B.C., or earlier. Sporadic construction of stone structures dates back to various periods assigned by archaeologists to Maya development. Structures pre-dating Late Classic times tended to be low profile and were made of rough-shaped blocks of stone which were plastered to cover rough areas and which used earth and loose stone material to fill interior voids.

Pyramid I (called the Temple of the Giant Jaguar) commands the east side of the Great Plaza. It is 145 feet high and contains the grave of an important ruler beneath an underground room.

At approximately 600 A.D. a change occurred in the masonry being used, and new construction methods emerged, resulting in a great surge of building activity which abandoned earth-bound confines and soared into the sky. This innovation, which marked the beginning of the Late Classic period, produced about 90% of all of the construction at Tikal from its founding until its demise sometime after 900 A.D.

The visible structures which we observe today at Tikal were almost all built during the Late Classic era.

The Maya followed a peculiar ritual, if the latter word can be used somewhat cautiously, in that many Late Classic structures were built upon the remains of earlier buildings. Quite often, archaeologists have found older buildings razed and their stone-work leveled and used as foundation material for a new structure; at other places, existing ruins were filled with rubble in order to provide a foundation for structures placed on higher elevations. Rarely do we find an older structure that has been repaired or renovated; and it is equally unlikely that there will or can be found instances where an older structure was completely removed to make way for a new structure in its place. The foregoing practice was not uniform, however, since there are instances (one being the Pyramid of the Magician at Uxmal) where rooms were retained intact and a superstructure was continued to a higher elevation. The habit of building upon the ruins of old structures suggests a possible tie to a religious practice common everywhere across the Yucatan Peninsula.

Tikal is distinguished among the great ceremonial centers by its great mass of stone structures, the relative abundance of stelae having "long count" dates and hieroglyphs carved on them, and a striking absence of mosaics of the kind common to Uxmal and other centers. It should be noted that a number of burial remains and caches have been found beneath various structures, indicating the existence of permanent habitation over a period of several hundred years.

Before proceeding further, it should be clearly understood that I did not come to the Yucatan Peninsula without having arrived at an opinion as to how the Maya could have worked the relatively hard limestone found in their structures. During the 12 years following my initial visit to Chichén Itzá and Uxmal, the matter preyed on my mind, and I was always probing every available source of information for an answer. After visiting numerous quarries east of the Mississippi River and contacting various quarry operators, I felt that I had developed sufficient facts to warrant further investigation.

It is well known among stone quarriers that limestone freshly ex-

A carved stela.

posed from many deposits is "green," bearing in mind that the use of the quoted word refers not to the color of the stone, but to its hardness. More specifically, when some limestones are removed from beneath the surface of the earth we find the stone to be relatively soft. After being exposed to sun, air, rain and other elements, those limestones gradually harden. With a knowledge of this common phenomenon, I concluded that the Maya possibly could have located large deposits of limestone and, after breaking through the upper crust, they could have shaped and trimmed individual smooth-faced building blocks with flint, bone or even limestone cutting tools in somewhat the same manner as peeling a carrot or potato. If such could have been done, the passage of time would have imparted a hardness to stone blocks which were soft when made. The theory was interesting, but the facts might not support it.

My first encounter with hard limestone was at Chichén Itzá, and it was my intention when I returned to secure the use of some drilling equipment and a backhoe so as to conduct a few experiments in the general area. However, as we were leaving Tikal I was beginning to realize that the matter was not as simple as I had hoped since other problems were presenting themselves. I was becoming confounded by mysteries compounded.

25

After leaving the high country north of Guatemala City, and before reaching Tikal, it became apparent that the westerly flow of moist Caribbean air across the hot lands of the Peninsula soon caused a low cloud cover to form. We had the choice of climbing on top and thereby seeing nothing, or flying beneath the clouds; we chose the latter and flew under the clouds at an elevation of less than 1,000 feet above the jungle so as to observe unearthed or partially excavated ruins along the way.

The problem of establishing proper headings and identifying our position was no simple task because we were flying too low to contact radio navigational facilities which would have been available at a higher altitude. As far as the eye could see there was nothing but green jungle beneath us, with not so much as a trail or stream to give us a clue to our position. We could only rely on the plane's compass, and so we took a general heading from Tikal toward Mexico's port-of-entry at Chetumal, not daring to take our eyes off the compass for even short intervals because the plane would tend to veer off course in the absence of landmarks to follow. There was also the distinct possibility that we might drift a bit to the right and end up flying illegally into Belize. The realization that our lives depended on a motor and a single propeller, knowing that a forced landing in the jungle would hardly generate any intensive rescue attempt, provided both of us with unspoken concerns as to why were we flying around over such a god-forsaken wilderness.

By setting a 25° compass heading and following small rivers which began to form as we proceeded northeasterly out of Guatemala, we eventually arrived at Chetumal, Mexico. All rivers ran into Chetumal Bay.

At Chetumal we rented a car and drove 30 miles inland to the ruins at Kohunlich. Our next flight on the following day took us up the coast of the Carribeo to Tulum, the fortress-like settlement built by the Post Classic Maya on a bluff overlooking the sea. We made a brief stop at Tulum and then proceeded by bus to Cobá, which is about 30 miles inland, where we spent most of another day examining those ruins.

None of the three last-mentioned sites, to which reference will be made later, shed any light on the question of how the Maya were able to work their stone; in fact, not one of those ruins produced any substantial evidence of precision stone-work of any kind. The stone used at all three sites was hard, irregular-shaped limestone pieces and chunks which for the most part had been secured from surface sources. Only a very small amount of stone at the three locations appeared to have been quarried, and very little of it had been worked into designs or shaped pieces for building purposes. The tendency in the general area leaned toward the use of mortar and plaster, which was understandable in view of the poor stone available for use.

Kohunlich, Tulum and Cobá were all located where one would expect to find better living conditions for people following farming, fishing and trading pursuits. And yet, the quality of the stone structures at all three sites was decidedly inferior to the construction found at Chichén Itzá, Uxmal and Tikal. Another frustration was added to my personal list of problems because it was becoming evident that the most beautiful stone structures with the best workmanship were found where people were least apt to live, but in areas where it appeared that life would be easier, poor-quality stone structures were the rule.

CHICHÉN ITZÁ and UXMAL

THE INLAND
YUCATAN PENINSULA
(shaded)

Dzibilchaltún
Merida
CHICHÉN ITZÁ
Cancún
Coba

Mayapán
UXMAL
Kabah
Sayil
Tulum
Cozumel
Labná

GULF OF
MEXICO

MEXICO

Becan
Chetumal
Kohunlich
Villahermosa

PALENQUE
El Mirador
Uaxactún
TIKAL

CARIBBEAN
SEA

BELIZE

MEXICO
Yaxchilán
Bonampak
Lake Petén

GUATEMALA

Quiriguá

COPÁN

Guatemala City

HONDURAS

PACIFIC
OCEAN

EL
SALVADOR

Chichén Itzá and Uxmal are the most famous ruins of the northern Yucatan.

OPPOSITE: Pyramid of Kukulcan at Chichén Itzá.

CHICHÉN ITZÁ

Our flight path from Tulum took us northwesterly over Cobá, and from there we angled to a point where the main east-west highway arrived at Valladolid. We then followed the main road west to Chichén Itzá.

It was at this major group of ruins that I had previously examined the stone-work on the pyramids and temples and concluded that no people could have cut, chiseled and shaped each single block of facing stone that went into their structures. To have produced each stone from solid masses of limestone with stone tools, such as flint or other limestone, struck me as a prodigious and impossible task.

As we flew over the ruins preparatory to landing, I received a pleasant surprise. There, beneath the left wing of the plane, a bypass road in the initial stages of construction was being run around the northerly side of the ruins. We circled several times before landing, during which I made a mental note of all landmarks in the area. Instead of seeking equipment and special permission to conduct some drilling operations in the general vicinity, it seemed that luck was running my way and that the job was being done for me. My best estimate was that two or three days' work would be saved and that the job being done in the area was far more extensive than could be performed at a few selected and isolated spots.

The road-building project was in full operation not more than a thousand feet from the pyramid temple of Kukulcan. Had we arrived as much as a week earlier, or a week later, it is quite possible that this firsthand opportunity of examining recently exposed limestone

Aerial view of the north portion of the ruins at Chichén Itzá, showing the new bypass highway under construction (1979) slanting across upper portion of photo.

Large crawler tractor, with ripper attachment, dislodging caprock on 1979 highway project at Chichén Itzá.

features would have been denied. As the beneficiary of such good fortune, it was with keen anticipation that I looked forward to the following day.

(a) *A Theory Destroyed*

I awakened at dawn on January 30, 1979, and hastily dressed and left our room at the Hacienda. It took less than 10 minutes to walk to the road construction site, where the day's work had already begun.

The bypass road construction was proceeding from west to east around the ruins, and advance segments of the project had almost connected with the original highway. In the vanguard was a TD-25 International crawler tractor, equipped with a dozer blade in front and a large ripper behind, which was clearing trees and vegetation from the

Cross-section, showing caprock overlaying thick strata of breccia, a condition prevalent across much of the Yucatan Peninsula.

highway route. The machine would alternately clear brush, trees and soil with its blade and then go over the same area and attack the low ridges which dominated the terrain with its ripper, dislodging large, irregular chunks of surface stone. A seemingly endless series of closely spaced ridges, varying as much as 20 feet or more from the bottoms of the dips to the tops, constitutes a condition usually encountered over much of the inland Yucatan Peninsula. Although giving a level appearance from a distance or from the air, the terrain is as jagged as sawteeth.

Critical to understanding our story is the knowledge that a substantial portion the Yucatan Peninsula contains a surface layer of hard limestone, usually referred to as "caprock." This material is very rough and irregular in shape, and it can be found either in broken chunks or in solid form. Caprock layers will vary from a few inches to several feet in thickness, with substantial variations often occurring within short distances.

Beneath the caprock, and in some instances on the surface where caprock is absent, much of the Peninsula contains a loose, granular form of calcium carbonate material known as breccia, or "*sascab*," as the material is called by the Maya. The material is somewhat similar to a marl, and it is readily loosened with a dozer blade, a shovel, or even a more primitive digging tool. The caprock and the underlying breccia are both classified as limestone and have essentially the same chemical components.

Since the limestone of the Yucatan Peninsula is of organic origin, it can be rubbed, pulverized or otherwise broken down into a fine powder containing little or no grit. This is so notwithstanding its relative hardness. The limestone in its natural, unexposed state is cream-colored, but when subjected to the weathering effects of sun, rain and air, it usually turns grey, although the effects of weathering and the time of day can also make it appear black, golden or even silver, depending on the nature of the stone at a particular ceremonial center.

The TD-25 tractor was laboring under full throttle as large chunks of caprock were ripped loose along the route of the road. This was something I was not prepared to accept because I believed the caprock would be dislodged easily and that the ripper would thereupon cut a groove through the underlying breccia. Actually, in areas where there was exposed breccia, I was expecting it to be considerably harder and much more consolidated than it actually was. The two separate and distinct masses of limestone were not what I had expected to find. One thing, however, was certain: The unsolidified, soft, granular breccia lying beneath the caprock was most certainly not the source of the stone from which smooth facing stones were secured for constructing pyramids and temples.

I returned to the scene of the large tractor and its ripping operation for the purpose of examining the caprock which was being

Many miles of fences are constructed of waste caprock taken from the countryside.

dislodged. On testing the stone with the point of my knife, I found the newly exposed cream-colored material to be every bit as hard as the same grey material found on the surface, thereby proving to me that in its natural, unexposed condition it never was soft enough to be worked with tools made of bone, flint or other limestone. Exposing it to the air might cause it to harden somewhat — but not much. It was far too hard in its natural form to be worked with stone tools.

Despite the efforts of the large crawler tractor, it was evident that much of the thicker caprock along the road could not be moved by the machine itself. Its implacable adversary defied every effort to remove some of the stone deposits, and the limestone which was dislodged came forth in large, rough and irregular chunks. Certainly, Stone Age man could never have cut, chiseled and chipped that material into

A well digging project, using only picks and shovels, produced this pile
of soft, granular breccia.

square- or rectangular-shaped facing stones.

The disturbing impact of my early morning findings was
penetrating another area of my experience, and I became abruptly
aware of an even more unsettling conclusion: It would be practically
impossible to work caprock limestone of the type I had been examining
into shaped facing blocks even with the best carbide-tipped steel hand
tools on the market today. My early morning adventure was turning
into a mental disaster.

I continued to walk alongside the dozers, trucks and other working equipment, stopping at intervals to smile and wave at the local
workmen. OSHA and MSHA, with their regulations and inspections,
had not penetrated Mexico — and no one seemed to mind one bit. A

Road construction crew drilling caprock within 500 feet of the Temple of the Warriors.

little farther along I came upon a small drilling crew working hard spots in the caprock which were deeper and too hard for the TD-25 to handle. What I next observed was another surprise to add to my growing list.

The workers were engulfed in a commotion of dust and noise, busily drilling holes in the hard limestone with rotary drills being furnished air from a Chicago Pneumatic compressor. I walked over and watched the drillers' noisy activities, smiling at them as I inserted ear plugs which I use both when flying and when operating drilling equipment at my own quarry. The drilling operation was blowing large quantities of dust from the holes, thus proving that the limestone was fairly hard; and as replacement steel was inserted at intervals as the holes deepened, the outpouring of dust continued, giving no indication whatever that softer caprock stone was being encountered several feet below the surface. Had softer stone actually been present, the drill bits would have cut faster and there would have been less dust as the bits descended; actually, one would normally expect that any softer material which might have been encountered would have been somewhat more moist, thus causing the bits to jam and cease rotating.

I sauntered over by the driller and examined his drill steel. To my amazement, he was using Swedish drill steel with a carbide-insert bit. Carbide bits are customarily manufactured either as a part of the drill steel assembly or as separate units which are screwed on the end of a length of hexagonal steel having a hole in the middle for the passage of air. Each bit usually contains two or four hard carbide steel inserts having pointed ridges so as to facilitate rapid cutting of the stone as the hole is drilled. By comparison, carbide-insert bits give much longer bit life and withstand abrasive stones far better than ordinary steel bits.

The operation, almost within the shadow of the great Pyramid of Kukulcan, utilized ammonium nitrate pellets for blasting purposes. Although used primarily for farm fertilizer, when ammonium nitrate pellets are mixed with a small amount of diesel oil so as to make the mix "tacky," and then tamped into drill holes and subsequently triggered with a single stick of high-explosive primer dynamite, the resulting blast will break and dislodge large quantities of stone. Many quarries, including my own, utilize the foregoing method.

On continuing my examination of the dislodged stone along the highway project, and even beyond as far as the village of Pisté, there was not one stone brought to the surface which could have been cut, chiseled or shaped into a building facing stone or mosaic insert for the walls or facade of a building. The countryside caprock stone at Chich'en Itz'a, as well as at other sites on the Yucatan Peninsula, was too hard to be cut or chipped into large quantities of structural or ornamental stones by any means that I could determine.

Three hours spent on the road project that morning completely destroyed the theory I had long nurtured as to how the Maya were able to construct their imposing stone structures.

(b) *The Search for Clues*

By midmorning I had completed my intended investigation, and the disappointing findings suggested that the remainder of the trip might turn out to be that of an ordinary tourist taking a simple vacation. But the challenge which remained was something I could not cast aside without expending a reasonable effort. Having worked with geologists at intervals over many years, I concluded that a ground inspection of the general area might be advisable, and so I proceeded to enter the surrounding jungle. I followed winding trails, crawled through entangling vines and trees on my hands and knees and inspected ravines and other surface irregularities in the terrain surrounding the ruins — all to no avail. As might be expected, I was searching for those elusive "quarries" — holes in the ground, if you will — from which the Maya secured the great volume of stone that went into their structures.

The jungle had done a good job of hiding the geology of the area; my search failed to reveal depressions of unusual depth or excessive deviations from what appeared to be natural contours along the ravines. There was the further overriding knowledge that, while there was hard caprock of varying depths to be found almost everywhere, beneath it all was the granular breccia material. It was therefore only reasonable to assume that any abandoned quarry from which building blocks might have been secured would not be more than a few feet deep.

I eventually emerged from the jungle, hot, tired, dusty and empty-handed. As an experienced quarrier, I was stymied: Where were the quarries? The stone in the great structures had to come from somewhere. There was nothing to be seen in the general area of the kind of stone found on the facing blocks of the buildings and pyramids; on the other hand, the recently uncovered caprock and the breccia material found along the road project and in excavated holes around the area indicated that the color of that stone, as well as stones within the protected portion of buildings among the ruins which had not been exposed to the sun and weather, was exactly the same.

As I walked along the jungle trail, a native boy of about 12 years

The interior of the Bath House retains the natural buff-cream color of local limestone which has not been exposed to the elements.

of age came onto the same trail not more than 200 feet away. He was holding a large diamond-back rattlesnake by the head with a forked stick. The snake was at least four feet long and exhibited a half dozen or more rattles which it was shaking quite vigorously, even though barely alive. The boy would probably skin the reptile, and the meat could provide a few good meals; for my part, I vowed to discontinue crawling in the jungle on all fours.

In moments of frustration there is sometimes an inner urge to attribute such great construction activities to unknown forces, such as visitors from outer space. I was in no frame of mind to consider such a possibility, but by that time it was evident that the Maya did not find their building stone in any of the spots where I had been searching. One answer, of course, was that they might have hauled the stone from some distant location, although I failed to perceive why Chichén Itzá was a better location than any other at which to build a ceremonial center.

Many writers have faulted the Maya for not having invented the wheel, but this has never given me any real concern. The wheel would have served those early Americans to advantage mainly if it could have been utilized for hauling materials or people across a passable terrain. If they had been able to contrive and physically construct a vehicle with wheels, the exceedingly rocky and irregular terrain, coupled with an impenetrable jungle, would have rendered such a vehicle useless; in fact, it probably would have been an impediment in most areas of the Yucatan Peninsula, as well as in the steep, rugged mountains and valleys of most of Mesoamerica. The Maya constructed roads in some areas, called "*sacbeob*" or "*sacbes*," but most of the Peninsula and adjoining mountain areas would not have accommodated a road system with attendant problems of maintenance in a land of roots, vines and other jungle growth.

Nor did the Maya possess those so-necessary beasts of burden which would have transformed the wheel into a practical means of conveyance: no donkeys or burros, no oxen, no horses. Further, lacking bronze or iron with which to build axles and hubs, and without adequate sources of grease and lubricants, it is easy to understand why the Maya opted for the tumpline, placed across the forehead, and simple backpacking techniques.

My probings into the transportation problems encountered by the Maya inexorably directed my thinking in the direction of a rather simple, and yet most important, conclusion: Their pyramids and other stone structures must have been built and placed at locations where stone could be secured rather close by. This conclusion was to become increasingly more important as the pieces began to fit together during the next few days.

I returned to the Pyramid of Kukulcan and the Temple of the Warriors, with the mocking form of Chacmool impudently staring at me. Where had you come from, I pondered? And why would the Maya construct a pyramid? Of course, it has been well known that the Egyptians and others built pyramids, often to furnish burial tombs for their rulers, and the Maya were certainly no exception in this respect. Perhaps the pointed geometric form of the pyramid impelled ancient people to expend herculean efforts in building pleasant - appearing, though useless, structures; or maybe their construction was just another adult manifestation of a child's tendency to build with blocks. The truncated pyramids of the Maya, each crowned with a temple, served as religious shrines and as abodes for their gods; their other buildings and palaces also seemed equally or even better suited for the same purpose.

Might it just be that pyramids also served ancient people for an equally important and different purpose as an effective means of disposing of large quantities of waste stone for which they could find no other practical use? The thought was intriguing.

An unrestored portion of the Pyramid of Kukulcan reveals a veneer of finished stones laid over a mass of waste rubble rock.

One does not discuss any pyramid without comparing it to the great Pyramids of Giza in Egypt, and so I must digress a bit. Those Egyptian pyramids were built on a plateau which runs parallel to the Nile Valley several miles west of Cairo. We have been led to believe that each pyramid was constructed throughout of several million precisely fitted and carefully shaped blocks of limestone, but such is not the fact. It is true that the shield, or covering layer, of the two largest pyramids had once been covered with blocks of limestone that had been carefully quarried, shaped and fitted, but most of the interior cores of those two large pyramids consist of large blocks of limestone which were obviously fitted together as best they could be without having been subjected to any extensive shaping process. In other words, the bulk of the interior cores of those two pyramids consist of rubble stone, as we would classify it today.

The Carnegie Institution restored the Temple of the Warriors and the Pyramid of Kukulcan during the late 1920s and the early 1930s.

AT LEFT:
A section of the Ball Court wall displays a wide range of patterns on the level faces of the wall stones. Variations often exist on individual stones.

OPPOSITE:
Horizontal grooves created by water levels and erosion outline the vertical breccia banks of the Sacred Cenote at Chichén Itzá. Caprock, with an occasional showing of layered stone, can be seen along the upper rim.

Two sides of the Pyramid of Kukulcan were restored, complete with an exterior cover of smooth facing stones, and the other two sides were left in their weathered and aged condition. A short walk around the pyramid revealed that its core consists of a great mass of rough rubble stone, indicating that the pyramid was in large part the waste product — and possibly the principal result — of some large quarrying operation.

If, as most writers have suggested, each stone used by the Maya for facing blocks on their temples and pyramids had been separately cut, chipped and chiseled with stone tools from solid rock outcroppings, why would they have expended so much labor in creating so many stones having no pleasing shape or practical form? Since it appeared to me that fully 75% of the stone in all of the structures at Chichén Itzá was strictly rubble material, with the remaining 25% or thereabouts having been shaped into square or rectangular facing blocks, the inconsistency did not mesh with long-held theories attempting to explain

the source of the building stone and the method by which it was quarried.

A further examination of the facing stones on the pyramid and the nearby ball court revealed their smooth surfaces to be somewhat mottled or pitted. One would expect that if the faces had been chipped with flint or other sharp stones a somewhat general uniformity would exist, but such was not the case. Quite often, a section of vertical wall revealed facing stones where one stone had a pitted surface somewhat deeper and with larger individual pit marks than other immediately contiguous facing stones. Also, some facing stones were nearly smooth, except for a mottled and slightly wavy appearance across their faces. A closer inspection created a suspicion in my mind that the smooth facing on those building stones might not have been created by human hands after all. But how? Somewhere in the back of my mind the appearance of those wall facing stones was striking a responsive chord.

(c) *A Special Dispensation from Nature*

Although I was doing a fairly good job of investigating and analyzing, I could not seem to tie into a single lead which would explain the source of the great amount of stone used in the ruins. Just about the only thing I was sure of was that the stone had not come from a great distance. With no answer, and as the day was ebbing, I walked up the trail a couple of blocks to the north and seated myself by the famous cenote.

It may have been that the approach of evening sharpens one's physical reactions and mental awareness; or it may be that I had pursued the matter to the point where there was but one answer; or it may have been that one or two physical items around the top of the cenote area focused my thinking; at any rate, my mind suddenly spanned a distance of nearly 3,000 miles to that stone quarry in northern Utah where I had labored a substantial portion of my life, and the answers rushed forth, not one by one, but crowding and stumbling over each other in a flood which wiped away the questions that had tormented me for years. I was fully conditioned to accept the answers but, as so often happens, I was not at the time prepared to consider the ramifications of the discovery.

As I slowly walked back along the trail and saw the restored ruins of the Maya in a new light, I was able to visualize the initial discovery by the Maya of an extensive surface deposit of limestone, probably not more than six or eight feet in depth, spread across a low mound in the very same spot where I was standing among the ruins. And of most importance, they found the deposit to be unlike the ordinary irregular and shapeless caprock of the countryside in that it was layered. More specifically, the deposit contained horizontal layers of stone of differing thicknesses, with each layer being separated from the layers below and above by thin seams of soft interstitial material.

The intermittent seams of foreign material, which usually varied from approximately one-fourth inch to as much as two inches in thickness, had not consolidated with the limestone layers on top and below. On examination, the Maya found that they could insert stone wedges and pointed poles into the soft material in the seams between the layers and thereby pry loose slabs of stone as they worked down from the top of the deposit to where there was solid, dense bedrock (or, where no bedrock was present, to the softer breccia material) which, in modern parlance, is designated as the quarry "floor." But the most important thing they discovered was that, as each layer of stone was separated from its natural bed, both the bottom and top sides of each individual slab were usually perfectly level and smooth, except for a slightly mottled or pitted effect which was pleasing in appearance.

The gap had been finally bridged: The Maya discovered stratified limestone deposits which they were able to work with simple stone tools, and they constructed their magnificent structures on-site. In the process of quarrying the surface deposits the best stone was utilized for smooth-faced building blocks and similar purposes, and the rough rubble stone was used for fill in the cores of their buildings and in their pyramids. Except for abrading the stone blocks to eliminate rough spots, incising shallow carvings and making heads and designs, the Late Classic Maya expended no more than ordinary efforts in chipping, chiseling and cutting stone blocks.

The mystery of the source of the better stone which found its way into the finished structures of the greatest Maya ceremonial centers can now be laid to rest. In addition, once having found the answer to the source of their stone, the door is open to approaching and understanding other facets of Maya activity which have mystified scholars for many years.

The stone deposits at Chich'en Itz'a and Tikal both furnish indictions of layers being approximately 25, 19, 15 and 13 inches thick. In addition, the stone construction at "old" Chich'en Itz'a, located primarily in the south portion of the ruins, indicates the presence of stone layers which were thinner than 10 inches. The stone deposits at Chich'en Itz'a extended, at irregular widths, for a distance of well over a mile. In that distance one would normally expect some variations in the thickness of each layer of stone in a deposit, so we cannot be certain how many layers actually existed when they were created by nature's handiwork. It is my best estimate that there were probably not more than six or seven separate layers in the deposits at Chich'en Itz'a.

We can now see why there does not seem to be any determinable unit of measurement in Maya construction. With quarried stone slabs having various thicknesses, and because facing stones were made by a breaking process, the Maya of necessity made stones having sizes and shapes best suited to their available material and the physical means at their disposal for their production. It is not surprising that we find no standardized measurements in any of their construction.

The solution to the problem I was pursuing had taken on a new and different twist: Instead of providing an answer as to how the Maya might have been able to manually produce smooth facing stones for their buildings, the answer lay in the fact that a special dispensation from nature provided them with layers of stone having two naturally smooth sides, and it only required the application of breaking and trimming processes to form building blocks from the natural material. The solution was so logical and simple that I was upset with myself for having taken so long to solve it; yet, on reflection, I felt fortunate in being able to find the missing link so necessary to understanding some of the how, whys and wheres of Maya construction.

In retrospect, it is quite apparent that the real reason why the secret had eluded everyone for so long was that the Maya (and later the Toltecs at Chich'en Itz'a) quarried and utilized all of their available building stone, leaving very little direct evidence of the source of the material which went into their pyramids and temples.

Having had the benefit of previously studying conditions at Tikal and Uxmal, as well as having read extensively on the subject, it was understandable that almost all of the Peninsula contained a layer of hard, shapeless caprock and, immediately below it, vast quantities of the granular breccia material; but the availability of layered building stone deposits of good quality, so necessary to construct the greatest and most famous ceremonial centers, was something else. It was becoming increasingly evident that large stone deposits of the latter type were relatively few and were found scattered at random across the Peninsula.

Notwithstanding numerous assertions by almost every writer that the Yucatan Peninsula contained inexhaustible quantities of readily available building stone which could be easily cut into blocks, it became suddenly clear that they were collectively wrong; indeed, the type of limestone from which building blocks could have been secured was limited as to its availability. Looking at the situation on the Yucatan Peninsula as a late 20th-century stone quarrier, the entire region and its present limestone resources appears to me to be one of the least-likely spots where one could quarry and shape building stone blocks with either stone tools or metal hand tools.

In the process of breaking quarried slabs to produce blocks of building stone, a considerable amount of uncontrolled breakage resulted in the production of unusable and shapeless rubble stone. Since this material was not pleasing to the eye, the natural thing to do was to hide it some place, and that most logical place was in the core of a pyramid. That was exactly the same thing that happened with the two largest pyramids of Giza in Egypt since it appeared to me that the inner cores of those two structures were filled with large blocks removed from a thick layer of surface limestone found adjacent to those pyramids along the plateau on the west side of the Nile Valley. Those blocks, having been removed from stratified layers, were both too large and their shapes lacked sufficient symmetry to be used by the

Egyptians for utilitarian purposes.

It would constitute an impossible task to peruse the many volumes written about the Maya in an effort to determine how much analysis has been focused upon the subject of how they quarried and worked the stone which went into their great structures, but it would be expected that relatively little can be found. Once faulty assumptions are accepted and repeated over and over again, even though erroneous, they project themselves and die hard. Accordingly, it should be interesting to see what constructive thoughts others may have advanced; and as this book is being written more than six years later, I find some support from other sources.

In an article published in *American Antiquity* in 1957, J. Ogden Outwater, Jr. discussed "Pre-Columbian Stonecutting Techniques of the Mexican Plateau." His training and experience was that of a mechanical engineer, and the article was introduced with the statement that an approach to understanding the civilizations of Middle American people should be made through their stone-work inasmuch as that was where they left their greatest mark. He did not examine the Yucatan Peninsula sites of the Maya, but his study included the inland Mexican sites of Malinalco, Xochicalco and Mitla (near Oaxaca).

At all three sites Outwater struggled with the standard approach of trying to locate the typical "hole in the ground" quarry. At Mitla, after analyzing three possible sources of the volcanic-type trachyte stone used in its construction, he finally concluded, correctly, that the stone was secured from the crown of a hill immediately above the ruins. At the other sites he was unable to find the "quarries," but observed that the unusual locations of their structures near the crests of mountains or hills created a reasonable probability that nearby areas had to supply the material needed for construction.

He labored with the problem of coming up with an answer to the method by which the stone was worked into desirable shapes at all three sites, but it is apparent that in each instance he found a situation where in fact the ancients were dealing with layered stone deposits. At Xochicalco he noted that the stone was hard and dense with flat surfaces that had no curvature or waviness that could be measured with a hand scale, and he was surprised that no "tool marks or directionality (could) be detected on the surface of" the stones. Also, at the same site, he noted the "pock-marked appearance" of the flat stones on the pyramid. Outwater also recognized that all of the people of Mesoamerica possessed a source of knowledge concerning the working of stone which could have been called on at any location.

Had Outwater been able to visualize that in each instance those who built the structures had found layered deposits of building stone, which they used to the last piece, he could have simplified his analysis to show how easy it was to devise a system for breaking and trimming the layered slabs of stone into desired shapes. His work, though falling short of the ultimate answer, does furnish considerable comfort to someone like myself who has broken new ground in the same direction.

In an effort to find some assistance from those immediately involved in the restoration of some of the ruins, I happened upon a book published in 1931 entitled *The Temple of the Warriors*. This book was written by Earl H. Morris who, beginning in 1925 and for several years thereafter, was in charge of site operations in restoring the Temple of the Warriors at Chich'en Itzá for the Carnegie Institution. Morris was a very versatile individual and a man of many talents, being particularly adept at mechanical pursuits. His story of the restoration of that structure reveals the challenge of the undertaking and certain conclusions one would naturally form from intimately working with the stone on the project.

In the last 20 pages of his book, Morris summarized and suggested that the facing blocks placed on the columns and walls of the structure were shaped at the quarry ". . .*to a semblance of rectangular form*. . ." From this observation, coupled with his disappointment in failing to find many stone tools which might have been used for working stone, he reasoned:

> For the shaping of ordinary wall stones it would seem that
> the blocks were broken to pieces as best they could be,
> with a tremendous amount of wastage. The increments
> were abraded by pecking until one surface was practically
> flat, and as a last step came the trimming of the edges to
> produce an approximately rectangular outline for the faced
> surface.

The Ball Court (rear), the Temple of the Jaguar (center), and the Platform of the Tigers and Eagles (lower right).

Morris was right in suggesting that the wall stones were produced by a breaking process and that much wastage occurred; but, even though he briefly made a passing reference to the existence of a massive horizontal stratum of neighborhood caprock without cleavage planes and from which he felt most of the building stone had been secured, he was unable to perceive that the building stones were served up in semifinished form by nature, thus eliminating any need for "pecking" in order to provide smooth faces. His analysis was restricted to the observable caprock of the vicinity; he could not bridge the gap so as to visualize what had actually existed.

Considering the physical qualities of the caprock at Chichén Itzá and every possible means which may have been available to the Maya for breaking it in the absence of numerous breaks or cleavage planes, it is my considered opinion that no layer of stone, even having a smooth upper and lower side, could be broken down into any reasonable number of stones from which facing blocks could be made if the thickness of the slab exceeded a maximum of 18 or 20 inches. Thicker stones, if not discarded as waste, would have had to be pounded, abraded or otherwise reduced in size and further dressed in order to be worked into the building program.

Most of the caprock which covered the usable layers of stone in the surface deposits at Chich'en Itz'a was indeed massive, ranging from two feet to four feet in thickness and generally containing relatively few vertical-type cracks. Where caprock of that type appeared, the Late Classic Maya could not break it; for that matter, neither could they remove much of it in order to get at the good layered stone beneath.

Morris undertook to make calculations of the number of man-days necessary to produce the burned lime necessary for the mortar used and to haul materials from the "quarries" to the structures, but he backed away from any attempt to provide us with an estimate of the time that would have been necessary to manually chip and peck a level surface on the face of 25,000 stone blocks used on the Temple of the Warriors alone. He, too, felt the sources of building stone were ". . .present on every hand," mistakenly equating the observable local caprock with the real source of the building stone used in the temples and pyramids at Chich'en Itz'a. Ironically, when he sought evidence of caprock with smooth faces similar to the building blocks he had been working with, it was nowhere to be found. Nor was he able to locate the "quarries" so necessary to a complete understanding of what took place. Nevertheless, the contribution made by Morris has helped considerably in focusing on the unknowns in the equation we have been studying.

Neither those who restored the ruins of the Maya nor the archaeologists who have sifted through them for clues have been able to locate the quarries from which the Maya secured their building stone — nor can they be found. In the process of removing the layered stone from the mounds where it was found, the quarries — if they can be called such — were systematically obliterated.

A special dispensation from nature.

Watercolor painting by Jan Burke.

AN ERA OF NEW TECHNOLOGY

The Yucatan Peninsula was once submerged beneath a great, shallow sea where, over eons of time, small sea animals deposited their remains on its watery floor, creating substantial layers of material which eventually solidified into a rock which we now know as limestone. As sometimes happens, there were periodic interruptions in the growth of marine life due to the effects of temperature and nutrient variations and other occurrences common to the earth's history.

As the new limestone was being created, a unique thing happened in that, during temporary intervals when marine life was not being accumulated, small deposits of different substances dropped on top of each successive layer of marine matter as it was being built up from the sea floor. This latter occurrence was most important to our story since the final limestone deposit, consisting of several layers, became stratified, or, as stone people would say, it was "bedded." The final limestone deposit consisted of horizontal layers of stone of various vertical thicknesses, separated from each other by the layers of foreign material which did not weld or fuse with the limestone layers both above and beneath.

Many kinds of building stone have been created by metamorphic action whereby their forms and shapes have been changed by heat, moisture or great pressure. In the geologic process of creating quartzite, for instance, the pressure from vast quantities of overburden has been so great that any deposits of foreign material between the quartzite layers were often compressed to a hairline thickness which can only be seen on close inspection.

Limestone is cementitious by its very nature, and it is not unusual to find deposits of limestone which have solidified without being subjected to the metamorphic conditions so necessary to the formation of many other kinds of building stone. Accordingly, bedded-stone deposits can be found with thin, discrete layers of foreign material between the bedded layers. Such at any rate, was the nature of the build-up which occurred at the bottom of that ancient sea which is now the Yucatan Peninsula.

(a) *The Mounds*

In the course of geologic time, as the continental plates were bypassing each other and after the great mountains running down the spine of Mexico and Central America had been pushed aloft, the Yucatan Peninsula began to birth from the depths, exposing in the first instance the limestone layers which had been accumulating on the bottom of that ancient sea.

As the new land crept towards the sky, the waters refused to release their treasure, and the waves crashed and pounded against the newly exposed limestone with all their fury; the sea, like the jungle which would take its place, was a jealous mistress which had no intention of giving up easily what rightly belonged to it. As a consequence, the greater portion of the several layers of limestone, which appear to have been fairly uniformly spread across most of the Peninsula, was gradually eroded, and the angry waters returned it to the depths.

It may have been that certain areas were uplifted from the sea more rapidly than others, or there may have been other conditions affecting the newly exposed limestone, but the final result was that some isolated and scattered deposits of bedded limestone survived the attrition of the elements. Those deposits varied upwards from as little as five or six feet in depth, and each contained several separate layers of limestone of different thicknesses. As might be expected, the bedded deposits which survived were almost always found on mounds or ridges at elevations somewhat higher than the adjacent terrain.

(b) *New Engineering and Stone-Laying Methods*

For hundreds of years the Maya observed the layered deposits of limestone scattered about the Peninsula, and occasionally they built low structures and corbeled vaults with blocks and strips of stone pried loose from the various layers. The blocks always had two parallel flat sides, thus making it possible to form the walls of the structures by stacking them one upon-the-other so as to become bearing walls.

The foregoing construction method was subject to severe limitations because the two smooth horizontal sides of each stone were once again hidden from view when placed in the same position in the structures as that which they occupied in the quarry, leaving the rough ends and sides of each stone (which the Maya could not shape and trim properly) exposed to view. The consequence of the foregoing problem was that the volume of construction was limited at most sites.

Many of the structures built prior to about 550 A. D. by the foregoing process were subsequently razed and their stones were rearranged on-site so that another structure could be built upon the rubble of the earlier one. Archaeologists who have dug into various ruins confirm the existence of this practice. Masonry methods were typified by rough-faced blocks of stone, with loose dirt and broken stone rubble used to fill voids. Sometimes the structures were given a pleasing appearance by the application of thick coats of plaster to both interior and exterior wall surfaces.

In general, stone structures built prior to the Late Classic period did not have the beauty and symmetry of those constructed at a later date, and our main interest in the "old" method of construction is in tracing the pattern of growth and development which led up to the major changes and techniques that ushered in the Late Classic era.

As so often happens, great technological advancements often occur by combining two or more separate and independent developments. It was just such a combination of events and circumstances which enabled the Maya to utilize their bedded-stone deposits and to embark on a wave of construction activity across the Peninsula, leaving in its wake nearly all of the visible ruins we visit today.

The first major event — though rather simple by hindsight — occurred sometime around 600 A.D., as near as we can determine at this time, when some obscure workman literally turned the Maya world on edge. Specifically, he found a better way to break and lay a building stone, thereby setting the stage for a completely different engineering approach to pyramid and building construction.

Someone with a sense of proportion and beauty observed that the "old" construction method wasted a valuable source of ornamentation when the smooth faces of the quarried stone slabs were stacked upon each other and hidden in a wall, and he reasoned that the slabs could be broken, trimmed and abraded so as to produce square or rectangular faces from the smooth bedding planes. Then, instead of laying the smooth faces in a horizontal position where they would be buried and hidden from view, they could be turned on edge to become visible, vertical facing blocks for steps, pyramids and buildings. The novel idea probably wasn't so new; rather, it can be better characterized as an idea whose time had come.

But there was a hitch in the practical application of the idea because the method of breaking each stone left most of its other sides (except for the face) irregular, rough and extending away from the stone face at different angles. Thus, the advantage gained was almost entirely lost because the smooth, parallel top and bottom surfaces of the quarried slabs could not be used to produce bearing wall blocks un-

THE TECHNOLOGICAL CHALLENGE
FACED BY
THE STONE AGE MAYA

The availability of several bedded-stone deposists at various locations across the Peninsula —

Provided an available source of flat limestone slabs having a smooth face on both the upper and lower sides of each slab;

and,

In order to utilize the smooth faces of the quarried slabs, it was necessary to break them in a way which would produce stones having square or rectangular faces, thereby requiring the breaking process to commence at and concentrate on the smooth portion of the slab; however, this approach made it almost impossible to control the shape of each stone beyond its smooth face;

and,

The problem encountered in placing the stones in a vertical wall (where their smooth faces were then 90° from the horizontal position where they reposed in the quarry deposit) mandated that some means be devised whereby the rough-sided blocks of stone — which could not be free-stacked — could be anchored and embedded into the wall structure.

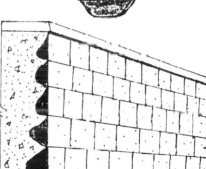

57

til some means could be devised to anchor the irregular-shaped blocks into or against the exposed portions of building walls or other structures. Fortunately, the solution had been available for a long time.

(c) *The Greatest Discovery of the Maya*

The Maya utilized the zero in their mathematical computations, they developed a calendar equal to or better than that created by any civilization on earth, and they came remarkably close to developing a written glyph system of writing. For all of the foregoing achievements their civilization has been justly cited. But there was another achievement of that remarkable people which, although taken for granted and sometimes discussed in a general way, was by far their greatest practical discovery. Had it not been for that important discovery and the role it played in enabling the Maya to adapt to the resources available to them — and even with full recognition being accorded the special bedded-stone deposits made available by nature for their use — the great ceremonial centers of the Yucatan Peninsula never could have been constructed:

> The Maya discovered cement and its application in making concrete, mortar and plaster.

The availability of concrete provided the technological climate which introduced the Late Classic era and its "Puuc" (sometimes called "florescent") style of architecture. The greatly expanded ability to introduce a broad variety of new and different designs and other forms of ornamentation provided a fertile field for architectural expression which had previously been held in check due to the limitations of available building materials. Along with the flexibility which the Puuc system of construction provided, we find at all of the major ceremonial centers under discussion the introduction of "foreign" Mexican influences on architectural styles. The Golden Age of the Maya was launched.

Henceforth, Maya construction, like that of the Romans, would consist of relatively thin ornamental facings superimposed over masses of interior rubble.

The art of producing concrete, mortar and plaster required little special ingenuity once cement became available. Of particular importance to our analysis, vertical walls utilizing the natural, smooth faces of quarried building blocks could be constructed by inserting a concrete mixture behind the vertical faces of the stones, thereby filling interior spaces where less-than-90° angles were present. This enabled the finished wall to constitute a solid mass of concrete-and-stone, with the decorative stones being embedded, or "veneered," into the total concrete structure. As might be suspected, the veneered stones had narrow, horizontal edges along the faces which rested upon the row of stones immediately below, and because of such fact the use of veneered stones served an entirely different structural function than stones which were used for bearing wall purposes.

It will be helpful at this point to set forth a few general definitions necessary to our discussion, not all of which are always clearly understood. Emphasis will be placed on their application to the resources and techniques available to the Maya:

CEMENT was the magic powder created by burning (calcining) limestone so as to create a chemical product which formed a bonding agent when mixed with water and various particles of matter.

CONCRETE was the solid mass which resulted from mixing cement with water and aggregates, usually other unburned limestone chips and smaller chunks of limestone, and then allowed to harden; its use was primarily devoted to creating the solid structural components of their palaces, pyramids and certain other buildings.

MORTAR was the bonding medium created by mixing cement with water and fine unburned limestone having a consistency similar to sand; upon hardening it served as a thin, compact bonding material which held larger stones together.

PLASTER, although similar to mortar, was usually made of "slaked" lime cement, with other substances often being added, thereby making it "pasty" and workable so as to provide smooth finished surfaces for walls, ceilings and floors.

Portland cement has sometimes been referred to as the miracle building material of the 20th century. This cement derived its name from the color of the limestone deposits at Portland, England, and it was discovered and perfected in England and France in a series of steps during the 1800s. Portland cement is made by combining and mixing limestone, silica, alumina and iron oxide, and then passing the mixture through a rotating kiln where sintering temperatures of 2800° Fahrenheit change the mixture into a hard clinker. The clinker is later re-ground to cement fineness and mixed with gypsum (so as to retard the setting process), and it is then ready for use. Limestone is the chief ingredient in the mix, with all of the ingredients being chemically and physically controlled within rigid limitations so as to make the best available product.

Prior to the 1800s and back to the time of the Romans, people often relied upon stone blocks for the wall components of many of their buildings, as well as for streets, curbings, sidewalks and the foundations of almost all major structures. The Romans, however, discovered and developed the art of making cement, and they have been recognized as the first people to use substantial quantities of concrete for construction purposes.

The Egyptians and other ancient peoples produced limited quantities of plaster which they used to cover and decorate the interior walls of their buildings, but it was not until the time of the Romans that we find cement used extensively for basic construction. The Romans were practical people and they adapted their building methods to available sources of building materials, including limestone, travertine and marble — all of the designated substances being calcium carbonates. They found they could burn limestone and add pozzolana (a red volcanic earth) to it, thereby producing a good cement. In fact, with the superior cement produced today by sophisticated procedures, we find that one part of pozzolan (which is not cement but which is usually fly ash secured from the smokestacks of coal-burning power-generating plants) can be mixed with four parts of cement, with the combination being at least equal to, and for some purposes better than, a straight mixture of five parts of cement. At any rate, by about 150 B.C. the Romans were making concrete with their cement, and building construction increased greatly.

From available evidence it appears that the Maya discovered cement and began to use it to make plaster at least as early as 500 B.C.

The reader might wonder what is so special about cement. Well, cement might be best understood by referring to it as very much a chemical product caused by burning certain raw materials at high temperatures so as to effect both chemical and physical changes. The Maya lacked silica (sand) and gravel, the silica being essential to the making of modern Portland cement, but they did have large amounts of limestone, and they made a good cement from their available materials. Since limestone is primarily calcium carbonate ($CaCO_3$) in composition, and also somewhat cementitious by nature, the Maya learned that they could burn that material and secure a powder which, when mixed with water and aggregates, would produce a good concrete. We know that when a certain quality limestone is burned a powdery and highly reactive quicklime is produced. It is the quicklime, and any complex silicates and aluminates it might contain, which gives the material its bonding properties.

The Simplified Cement-Making Formula Used by the Maya

(1)   Natural limestone breccia and
      chunks (calcium carbonates) . . . . $CaCO_3$

(2)   were burned in an open-air kiln,
      driving off carbon dioxide . . . . $- CO_2$

(3)   and leaving a residue of lime
      cement (calcium oxide) . . . . CaO

The cement produced by the Maya was more nearly the equivalent of modern masonry cement, and it was calcined and burned at

Cement-making was accidentally discovered by burning limestone in camp fires. Stylized sketch by Jan Burke.

temperatures in the range of 1,800° Fahrenheit. Most of the limestone used did not contain significant amounts of alumina, iron oxide or silica.

We might wonder how the Maya discovered cement and, for that matter, why they eventually used it in concrete construction. In this respect, some of the statements of the archaeologists and writers are correct because there truly was an abundance of cement-making materials on every hand. Limestone, particularly the caprock and the underlying breccia, was literally underfoot across most of the Yucatan Peninsula. We only need ask whether the discovery of cement resulted from an unlikely accident or if it might have been unavoidable.

We can visualize a group of hunters in the jungle of the Yucatan Peninsula stopping at a campsite and, as night descended, building a fire to ward off mosquitos and to cook a meal from the day's hunt. As hunters always do, the fire was placed between chunks of limestone (there being no other durable rock in the entire area), and the bed of the fire may have consisted of granular breccia material. If a few pieces of hardwood had been available, the ensuing fire would have burned long and hot during the evening hours.

After the fire died out and the embers cooled, the hunters would have noticed that the breccia in the bed of the fire, together with a portion of the blocks containing it, had pulverized from the heat and turned to a white ash-type substance. And it would only be fair to expect that at times a few small chunks of hard limestone would have been tossed into the powdery remains of the fire after it had gone out and the ashes had cooled.

When the hunters returned to the same spot after the lapse of several days and an intervening rain, they would have found the ashes at the site of their fire to have been puddled and hardened into a solid mass, surrounding and containing the chunks of limestone which had been added to the dry ashes with a bond that could not be easily broken. From this and numerous other similar incidents which occurred at various places, the discovery of cement by the Maya would have been inevitable.

The Maya did not understand the chemistry of making cement, but they did know that something took place in the burning of the limestone which produced the powdery substance that held their world together. But there was a major obstacle to overcome, since the paltry amount of cement produced by a campfire process was totally disproportionate to their needs if they were to construct elaborate ceremonial centers with the bedded-stone deposits available for their use. What they needed was the equivalent of a massive metal kiln which would achieve high burning temperatures and distribute the heat throughout a large quantity of limestone chunks so as to effect uniform burning and the production of a substantial quantity of cement.

The Maya rose to the occasion and, with no metal and notwithstanding the fact that their only available stone would pulverize if

63

exposed to fire, they built a kiln which exhibited a superior knowledge of the principles of physics. The recognition by the Maya of the amazing qualities of cement can properly be considered a discovery; the remarkable method they devised to create substantial quantities of cement was their invention.

A kiln is essentially a special kind of furnace wherein both temperature and burning time are controlled by regulating the amount of air being fed to the fuel. Modern cement kilns utilize this procedure by directing a blast of fire against a constantly moving mixture of raw materials, thereby subjecting it to complete burning; and the carbon dioxide which is burned off is discharged through a vent which draws the gas upwards into the atmosphere. The Maya burned limestone and made cement by an ingenious single-stage production process utilizing an open-air kiln.

The first step in the process involved setting a wooden pole of approximately 10 feet in height and eight or ten inches in diameter upright in the middle of a smooth, level, cleared area, and then placing a small pile of dry, flammable material around the pole. A circle was drawn on the ground, and the remainder of the area, which extended radially a distance of approximately 10 or 15 feet or more from the center, was carefully filled and stacked horizontally with the trunks, branches and small limbs and twigs of green hardwood trees which were cut in the vicinity. The larger trunks and branches were placed around the circumference of the circular affair, pointing inward; also, larger trunks and branches were placed across the entire bottom layer, pointed towards the center pole so as to permit outside air to be drawn inwardly to the center of the pile and then up the vent created when the pole was later removed.

Successive courses of green hardwood material were laid horizontally and stacked tightly, with the larger trunks and branches always being placed around the perimeter of the circle and the thinner and shorter branches, limbs and twigs being placed nearer the center, to a height of six feet or more. Finally, a layer of broken limestone, usually consisting of breccia and chunks six inches or less in diameter, was placed upon the mass of green limbs, branches and trunks. The limestone ''lid'' was usually about two feet thick and the diameter of the mound

A pile of small limestone chunks and limited amounts of granular breccia
was placed on top of a large cylinder of green tree trunks, branches and limbs. The
center of the pile was fired and, after burning, there remained a pile of lime cement.

of stone was about three or four feet less than that of the underlying
pile of green hardwood.

The pole in the middle of the round, compact mass would be
removed, and the dry material located at the bottom of the hole where
the pole had been located was then fired when a calm day was
available. A strong updraft soon produced a dense, white smoke as the
green material ignited, but this settled down to a very hot, pale-blue,
steady flame in a short time. Green wood was always used because it
burned both slower and hotter. The total mass would burn for two or
three days, with the bottom center area burning first. As the burning
progressed, the top center area would gradually settle and sink as the
fire consumed the green hardwood, and the process would gradually
extend outward as the burning eventually reached the outer edge of
the stack of wood.

After the fire had burned out, there remained a mound of white
lime cement (CaO) which was available for making concrete, mortar or
plaster. The use of fresh lime cement causes plaster to crack and pro-

duce check marks, so the Maya found that they could take some of the cement and slake it by periodically exposing it to rain or small amounts of water, thus causing it to swell to several times the size it occupied in the mound after the burning had been completed. The slaked lime cement (calcium hydroxide — $Ca(OH_2)$) was mixed with unburned powdery breccia in the ratio of about one part cement to three parts of natural breccia. The water for the mixture was often allowed to soak up chemicals from the bark of the chocom tree, thus causing the mixture to produce a superb polish, without checking, as well as imparting a bright red finish. As a hard surface finish, the lime cement plaster was very moisture resistant.

An analysis of a solid piece of mortar used on the structure at Sayil which introduces the final chapter on "The Collapse" shows the following:

SiO_2	3.20%
Al_2O_3	0.08%
Fe_2O_3	0.85%
CaO	51.45%
MgO	0.98%
Na_2O	0.16%
K_2O	0.24%
Loss on Ignition	43.04%
Total	100%

It will be noted that the percentages of sand (SiO_2), alumina (Al_2O_3) and iron (Fe_2O_3) constitute less than 5% of the ingredients and that limestone (before burning) represents nearly 95% of the total. Further, since magnesium oxide (MgO) is only about 1% of the total, the limestone used at Sayil was not dolomitic; rather, it would be classified as a very good grade of limestone ($CaCO_3$). In fact, the very best limestone upon burning (Loss on Ignition) will yield 56.00% CaO. Since there was less silica (SiO_2) than might be desired, the resulting mix, although somewhat deficient in strength, produced a very adequate pasty cement substance for bedding and binding stones together.

During the lapse of approximately 1,000 years since the structure was completed, the presence of jungle growth and humid air has allowed carbon dioxide (CO_2) in the air to gradually penetrate the mortar and combine with the calcium oxide (CaO), thereby reconstituting calcium carbonate ($CaCO_3$) by the process of re-carbonization. Thus, nature by its own processes took over after man abandoned the scene and slowly restored its substances to their original condition.

Most of the Yucatan Peninsula did not contain sand and gravel as aggregate material to mix with the lime cement, so concrete was made by mixing lime cement with the native granular breccia and smaller pieces of limestone which were produced when slabs of layered stone were broken during the quarrying and finishing process. By utilizing the same general rule-of-thumb standards applicable today, the concrete in the veneered facing walls used approximately one part of lime cement to four or five parts of aggregate material. For the concrete in the cores of the pyramids and buildings, a less-rich mixture of one part of lime cement to six or more parts of aggregate material was probably used, depending upon the structural strength desired at a given point.

Shortly after I published my basic treatise *The Maya — A Legacy in Stone*, an interested correspondent sent me a copy of an article published in the 1965 Winter issue of Southwestern Journal of Anthropology entitled *Monument Building: Some Field Experiments*. The article was authored by Charles J Erasmus, and it contains several interesting observations concerning building practices of the Maya, and in most part I concur. He opined that their monument construction could have been performed by people at a "chiefdom" level of socio-political integration without there having been a centralized political organization and that the amount of labor necessary to construct a ceremonial center was probably less than had been suggested. To support his thesis he conducted some experiments with present-day Maya workmen to determine the man-days necessary to pry loose and manually haul local caprock in the vicinity of Tikul (which is just over the Puuc hills from Uxmal) to specified distances. From these experiments he concluded that the man-days required to move stone in his experiments were greatly affected by the distance between the point of excavation and the placement of the fill, and he summarized with an opinion that the Quadrangle at Uxmal could have been built in a little more than 13 years under normal conditions and as little as seven years if the project had been pushed. Understandably, the time frame necessary to construct the Quadrangle would have been greatly influenced by the number of workmen engaged in the project and the available working days per year when construction could have proceeded.

Erasmus avoided the issue of how much labor would have been required to shape and face the caprock into building stones (assuming that it could have been done), not suspecting that the Maya actually were working easily quarried bedded-stone deposits. Had this information been available to him, it is entirely possible that he might have shortened his estimates of the time required for the construction of the Quadrangle.

Perhaps the most interesting feature of his study pertains to information he received concerning the method of creating lime cement from the burning process I have just outlined. He was furnished figures indicating that a stack of 12.5 tons of limestone rock and just under 7.00 tons of green firewood would produce 8.25 tons of burnt lime.

The figures quoted by Erasmus indicate that for each 1.5 ton of stone there would be 1.0 ton of lime cement produced, thus giving a percentage weight of burned lime cement to the raw limestone placed in the open air kiln of 66.7%. In the simplified formula previously set forth, we know that lime cement is created by burning away carbon dioxide (CO_2) from calcium carbonate ($CaCO_3$), leaving calcium oxide (CaO). In this chemical process, it should be understood that the carbon dioxide which is burned off is not simply weightless air — it is very much a loss of physical weight. In making Portland cement today by burning the carefully controlled mix which is fed into the fired kilns, we find an almost identical result occurring: For each 1.5 ton of raw material fed into the kiln there can be expected to be produced nearly 1.0 ton of cement. The comparative percentage, subject to a few complex variables which need not concern us here, generally runs between 62% and 66%.

The Maya did not have the range of secondary raw materials available for a sophisticated cement mix, and their burning process was less efficient than that which we now employ, but the present condition of their plastered walls and the cores of their structures, some of which are more than 2,000 years old, attests to their manufacturing skill and the quality of their lime cement.

(d) *The "Corbeled" Arch*

Numerous writers have slighted the Maya by asserting that they were unable to master the art of building the Roman arch. This is an unfortunate and incorrect indictment, particularly since those commentators have been insufficiently informed. In this area, too, there has been a failure to examine the matter in depth.

The Roman arch has generally been considered a triumph of engineering skill, providing a method of spanning doorways and enclosed spaces, city gates, bridges and aqueducts. One of the most notable examples is the massive aqueduct at Segovia, Spain, built about 100 A.D., the arches of which were made of cut granite stones

LEFT: The Aqueduct at Segovia, Spain.

BOTTOM: The bridge across the Tagus River at Alaćantara, Spain.

closely fitted against each other without any bonding material. Another well-known example which still stands is the high bridge across the Tagus River at Alacantara, Spain.

The true arch is a curved lintel with each stone or brick being wedge-shaped and having two converging sides, with the narrow portion of each stone or brick being at the bottom of the arch, thus causing the weight of the arch and any superimposed mass to press the stones or bricks together. The natural result of the combination of lateral thrust (outward pressure) and vertical thrust (downward pressure) creates a diagonal thrust which pushes against the supporting bearing walls on each side, and if not supported by buttresses, the entire structure will collapse and fall. The answer to the problem was to construct thick bearing walls (buttresses) capable of withstanding the pressures involved, and it was for this reason that the Roman arch was so well-adapted to span across canyons or ravines where sloping, natural sides would absorb the ever present diagonal thrust forces.

The Maya were working with stone slabs having two parallel smooth sides; and because they lacked metal tools, it would have been very difficult to produce the wedge-shaped stones necessary to construct the arch. The alternative was to lay overlapping flat stones in successive, horizontal layers, with each layer extending inwardly and beyond the prior layer as each side of the vault proceeded upwardly to where the span could be joined by a single stone across the top. The method employed to offset problems associated with thrust was to counterbalance both sides of the vault with a large mass of material above and on either side so as to shift the center of weight of each half of the vault outwardly to a point more nearly above the bearing walls.

As a practical matter, however, both the Roman arch and the corbeled arch of the Maya had severe limitations in that they could not adequately handle the problem of diagonal thrust, and it was because of that inherent defect that we find relatively few true examples of either arch where large spans were bridged or where substantial weight was supported above and by the arch.

The Roman arch was not used extensively until about 150 B.C., at which time the Romans developed the art of making cement and

Two high, open vaults are keys features of the Palace
of the Governors at Uxmal.

building with concrete. By bridging the arched span between the supporting columns with a solid mass of concrete, the problem of lateral
thrust was nullified and the entire weight then bore straight down on
the bearing walls or columns, which were made of stone blocks, brick
or concrete. Having found this solution, it was a simple matter to
veneer the arch stones against and into the concrete mass behind them.

As a result, the functional effect of the visible components of the
Roman arch often became limited and, as a deceptive veneer, the value
of the arch was mostly cosmetic.

So, too, the corbeled arch had similar problems. As we have seen,
the limestone facing blocks created by the breaking process did not
produce the perfect right-angled blocks necessary to bearing wall
stability, so the Maya would have been stymied before they began

building construction. Even if the bearing wall problem could have been overcome, the overlapping vault stones laid flat upon each other would have seriously limited the width of the span which could have been bridged by successive layers of relatively flat stones.

The answer for the Maya was to do as the Romans did, and they solved their room-spanning problems by bridging the vault with a solid concrete mass. They then placed veneered facing stones against all inside walls of the pointed vault. A close inspection of the veneered facing stones in almost all of their remaining ''corbeled'' vaults makes it evident that the stones furnished little structural support; it was the large concrete mass located above and on both sides of the vault which held everything together. Likewise, concrete furnished the principal support for the bearing walls of most Late Classic temples and palaces.

During the Late Classic period, when most of the great structures were erected across the Yucatan Peninsula, almost all ''corbeled'' vaults were built by the concrete-and-veneer method. It would seem that the question of the utility of either type of arch has long been a moot issue since the use of concrete transferred the entire matter from the realm of engineering into the area of architectural effect. The Maya, like the Romans, were masters of deception — they both built magnificent edifices by ornamenting masses of concrete with beautiful veneers.

The Quadrangle and the Pyramid of the Magician at sunset.

NOTE: For location map of Uxmal see pages 4 and 28.

UXMAL AND OTHER PUUC CENTERS

A 50-mile drive south from Merida brings one to the Puuc Hills, and there we can observe the ultimate development of Maya architectural and construction skills. At no other location do we find so many distinctive and unique palaces and related structures. The Puuc Hills contained the premier stone deposits available to the Maya, and the quality and versatility of the stone enabled their architects to perfect the use of mosaic patterns, to create interesting and pleasing building styles and to adorn their structures with designs which are seldom found elsewhere. Although the construction of pyramids was continued in the region, it strikes one forcibly that there, as at no other place, pyramids were really by-products of sophisticated quarrying and construction activities.

The south complex at Uxmal, consisting of (left to right) Palace of
the Governors, the Great Pyramid (unrestored), the House of the
Turtles and the Dove-Cote.

The Puuc ceremonial centers, nearly all of which are spaced within
a distance of 30 miles extending southeasterly from Uxmal, contain a
collection of at least a half-dozen pre-Columbian architectural master-
pieces of the New World, all of which adopted and perfected the
veneer method of stone construction. For reasons which will be apparent as our discussion proceeds, construction at the Puuc sites was
concentrated near the end of Late Classic times, and most of those
ceremonial centers fell into decay within a short time after their completion.

(a) *A Region of Ridges and Mounds*

The Puuc Hills lie at an elevation of about 400 feet above sea

East end of House of the Turtles.

level, and it is in that rolling and varied terrain where we find the
ceremonial centers of Uxmal, Kab'ah, Sayil and Labn'a. On approaching Uxmal there can be observed two main clusters of pyramids
and buildings, one group being located on the north ridge of a wide
ravine and the other group being located on the south ridge. In the
background there are several smaller mounds which have been quarried, each with its own individual group of structures. I eyeballed the
entire complex and concluded that, while there may have been a
limited amount of "platform building" to accommodate the placement of certain buildings, it appeared that most of them were placed
entirely or in large part on a solid limestone base after all usable bedded stone had been quarried and removed from the site. Some of the
buildings were put at staggered elevations, suggesting that the floor, or
base, of the limestone deposit was located at different elevations. As
an example, the north building of the Quadrangle appears to have

The Palace of the Governors.

been placed on the floor of the highest deposit of bedded stone in the immediate area, and the other buildings were located nearer the plaza level about 15 or 20 feet lower.

All of the ridges and mounds in the Uxmal complex had been systematically quarried and the usable stone removed, furnishing perfect examples of worked-out stone quarries. As I walked among the restored ruins, I experienced the eerie sensation of being in the midst of one of the most glorious ghost towns on earth. It was a haunting thought to realize that the Maya quarried their available stone and used it for buildings and pyramids located on-site, whereas the miners in the western United States hauled the minerals away and used them at locations where people preferred to live. It is in the nature of things that the valuable minerals on this planet are usually found in isolated and inhospitable places.

Rear of the north building of the Quadrangle. The entire distance of nearly 280 ft. was elaborately decorated, even though the building was elevated and the rear portion was usually viewed from a distance.

The average Maya workman was probably little more than five feet in height, and it is unlikely that he was fond of hauling rocks on his back for great distances. At Uxmal, as at Tikal and Chich'en Itzá, the buildings were placed either directly upon or very near the exact spot where stone had been removed from the bedded deposits, and pyramids and platform areas were likewise located where stone hauling was reduced to a minimum. The rule-of-thumb standard for moving stone at all of the five major ceremonial centers under discussion was generally within a radius not exceeding 500 to 600 feet from the quarry source.

The mounds from which building stone was taken at Uxmal were located at elevations somewhat higher than adjacent areas, thus providing the Maya with an opportunity of simplifying the logistics of moving their rubble waste stone. Both the pyramid of the Magician (by the north complex) and the Great Pyramid (by the south complex) were located a short distance away from, and below the elevation of, the mounds and building area. This made it possible to bring some of the rubble stone for pyramid fill to the respective structures by packing the stones across a ramp or, if no ramp was used, by minimizing the net up-hill climb. Since pyramids converge rapidly at their apex, the amount of rubble stone which had to be carried to the maximum height was reduced considerably.

The Egyptian Pyramids of Cheops and Chefhren were constructed on the same principle in that both were located at a point on the plateau above the Nile Valley which dropped away from the higher area where the large blocks of limestone were found. In order to handle the larger limestone blocks used by the Egyptians, it was necessary to utilize ramps, but by being able to extend the ramps from the adjoining slope more nearly on an elevation with the stone deposit, the Egyptian pyramids received probably as much as 80% of their core material before it became necessary to do substantial battle with gravity. Of interest, my examination of the two pyramids of Giza suggested that the plateau deposit of limestone had been high-graded with the better quality stone having been used on Cheops, the larger pyramid, and that stone of generally lesser quality and smaller sizes was used on the Chefhren pyramid.

It would seem that our predecessors who worked with stone at any place on earth were keenly aware of their own capabilities and of the stone resources available for their use.

(b) *Efficient Construction Techniques*

Once we realize that the Maya could secure smooth slabs of building stone from layered deposits by prying and lifting them loose, and that it was only necessary to break the slabs and thereafter trim and abrade the edges around the stone faces so as to create square or rectangular blocks, an entirely new dimension of labor requirements presents itself. For more than 150 years the public has been fed a steady diet of pronouncements that literally thousands of workmen were involved in an anthill of activity over great periods of time in constructing each of the major ceremonial centers. Without belittling the efforts and achievements of the Maya, I am stating as a fact that the Maya were so efficient in quarrying and working their stone deposits that their manpower requirements were only a small fraction of what has been believed.

After the Maya removed the small amount of overburden which covered the stone deposits found on most mounds, a half-dozen workmen could insert sharp poles or drive wedges into the seams beneath the layers and thereby dislodge several tons a day. The next step required that the slabs be broken to produce square or rectangular faces, and this probably was done partly during the quarrying process and then completed after the broken stones were removed from the quarry to a work area. Although not always done, it would have been desirable to ''score,'' or edge, thin grooves in each limestone slab along the line of the desired break, much as a glass cutter makes a

Stone slabs could be quarried easily from bedded-stone deposits. Exposed side view of deposit shown. Stylized sketch by Jan Burke.

A heavy hardwood pole could break rough blocks from dislodged slabs, particularly if grooves were etched along the desired break-line. Side view. Stylized sketch by Jan Burke.

sharp indentation along the line of breakage. This procedure would have caused a clean break when pounding was applied to the stone slab.

We find that stone cannot be broken easily as it lies in its natural bed since the shock produced by pounding will be disbursed over the entire area where contact occurs. As proof, try dropping a flat stone into a bed of sand, and then try breaking the stone in some desired fashion. The result will be that the stone will break in every direction except that which is desired. To solve the problem the Maya soon learned that a stone could not be broken with any degree of accuracy until it became "vulnerable." Better illustrated, a slab of stone could be pried loose from its natural bed and raised a couple of inches; workmen would then insert small wedges between the layers back from the front or face of the stone the desired width of, say, 15 inches, thus leaving an extended piece of slab with no underlying support base to cushion the shock resulting from the blow from above.

The most-likely tool to make the initial break for producing facing stones from the thicker layers was a round post of green hardwood, usually weighing from 25 to 40 pounds, which could be raised and lowered with heavy, effective blows. Once a workman got the "feel" for the propensities of the stone and its reaction to his breaking tool, he could soon master the skill necessary to produce a large number of facing stones. We should not expect that every encounter produced a stone which could be made into a square or rectangular surface, but the workmen knew that all badly broken stone, or rubble, would be taken to a nearby pyramid.

Nor should it be thought that the breaking process always produced blocks of stone having breaks which were at right angles to the bedded faces, although for most uses it would have been a desired result. Actually, by far the greater number of broken stones would have had angles approximately 60° and 120°, respectively, extending away from the smooth bedding plane of the slab. This condition required a certain amount of simple chipping and abrading along the sharp (acute) edge of the broken stone so as to make a straight line and right-angled corners on the finished face of each stone. Further, a logical extension of the breaking process applied to each stone generally produced tapered rear portions. The finished stone blocks were often shaped like television tubes.

The use of concrete made it possible to erect

End section of wall at Uxmal, showing tapered facing stones set in concrete. Note the use of smaller, thinner stones at the top of the wall.

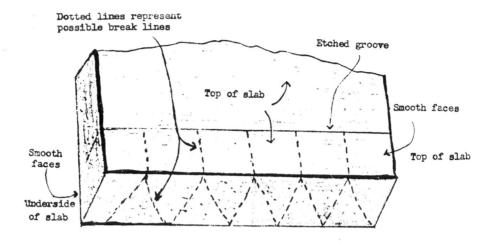

Dotted lines represent
possible break lines

Etched groove

Top of slab

Smooth faces

Smooth
faces

Top of slab

Underside
of slab

End view of quarried slab

The section of the slab interspersed with dotted lines could theoretically produce (from both bottom and top sides of the slab) 10 or 11 good-sized facing blocks; actually, because of cross-fractures and imperfections in many slabs, coupled with uncontrolled breakage, 3 to 5 good facing blocks and several smaller blocks for stair risers and other uses requiring smooth-faced stones would have been normal production.

structural walls with smooth facing stones which did not require substantial bearing surfaces extending inwardly at right angles from both the bottom and top horizontal edges of each stone. This resulted in a major departure from the older heavy-and-low type of construction to new and somewhat less bulky types of structures having thinner, more-symmetrical and higher exterior walls and vaulted rooms, and featuring facades and other areas with interesting designs and rich adornment.

In addition, an important side effect complemented the use of concrete in that the available bedded-stone deposits produced a much greater number of usable smooth facing stones than theretofore and, in the process, provided for a minimal (or at least tolerable) amount of waste material to be used as concrete aggregate and for the rubble core of pyramids.

To illustrate: A substantial portion of the bedded limestone came from layers which were from 13 to 20 inches thick. Inasmuch as each layer was provided by nature with a smooth horizontal top and bottom side, it was not imperative that a Maya quarrier should make a vertical break through the stone slab at a 90° angle since a break from either face of the slab at, say, a 45° angle would result in a reciprocal 45° companion angle on its adjacent side and, if the break was straight, similar angled breaks on the opposite horizontal side of the slab. Thus, maximum utilization of the two smooth surfaces of each stone layer could be had by breaking away desired portions and then turning the slab over and repeating the process on its other flat side.

It should be noted that the breaks on the horizontal surfaces of each slab would have had to be made so that, with additional trimming and abrading, square or rectangular faces could be secured. Also, since the shape of the slabs was rarely rectangular, the distance back from the face of the slab at which the vertical break was made presented an additional problem. Both of the foregoing conditions further limited the quantity of smooth facing stones which could be produced.

The Maya had no unions to delineate their activities, thus allowing for a great amount of overlapping activities, but we can form a reasonable estimate of the manpower necessary to constitute an efficient quarrying and construction crew at one of the larger ceremonial centers. To this end I have concluded that a work force of 200 men — not several thousand — working during a period of not more than 200 days per year, would have been ample and efficient.

The accompanying chart illustrates my analysis of the material-flow percentages and the number of workmen necessary to handle each phase of the operation.

The standard by which to measure the productive capacity of the 200 workmen in the illustrative chart is that of ascertaining how many square feet of exposed exterior and interior shaped or mosaic stone the

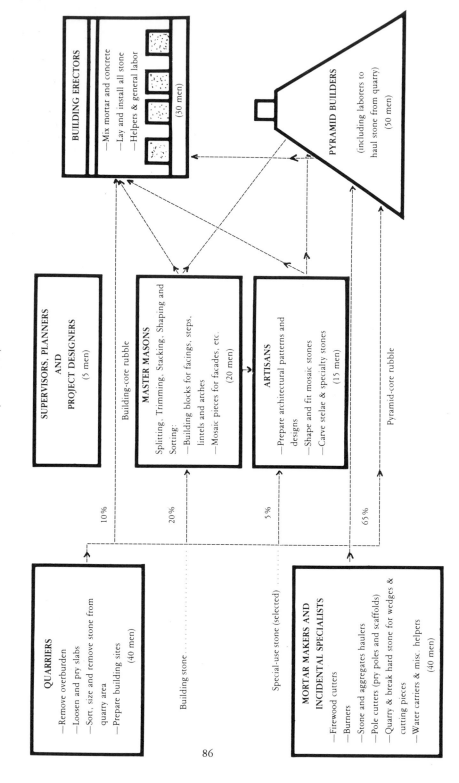

UXMAL
(200 man crew)

SUPERVISORS, PLANNERS
AND
PROJECT DESIGNERS
(5 men)

BUILDING ERECTORS
—Mix mortar and concrete
—Lay and install all stone
—Helpers & general labor
(30 men)

MASTER MASONS
Splitting, Trimming, Stacking, Shaping and Sorting:
—Building blocks for facings, steps, lintels and arches
—Mosaic pieces for facades, etc.
(20 men)

ARTISANS
—Prepare architectural patterns and designs
—Shape and fit mosaic stones
—Carve stelae & specialty stones
(15 men)

PYRAMID BUILDERS
(including laborers to haul stone from quarry)
(50 men)

QUARRIERS
—Remove overburden
—Loosen and pry slabs
—Sort, size and remove stone from quarry area
—Prepare building sites
(40 men)

MORTAR MAKERS AND
INCIDENTAL SPECIALISTS
—Firewood cutters
—Burners
—Stone and aggregates haulers
—Pole cutters (pry poles and scaffolds)
—Quarry & break hard stone for wedges & cutting pieces
—Water carriers & misc. helpers
(40 men)

Building-core rubble

Building stone

Special-use stone (selected)

Pyramid-core rubble

10%

20%

5%

65%

30 "Building Erectors" would have installed in a given day. By today's standards a single mason, with a helper, would be expected to install at least 50 square feet of such surface material a day, so 15 masons and 15 helpers sould install about 750 square feet per day. It is my estimate that the Maya workmen performing that job would have installed at least 150 square feet of vertical, finished stone-work per day after operations were in full swing as the end product of the efforts of 200 workers.

If a total labor force of 200 worked for 200 days each year, the four-building Quadrangle complex conceivably could have been put together in as little as 10 or 20 years, and they would have ended up with a pyramid as a by-product for good measure. We do not know whether all of the major ceremonial centers were pushed to completion during the Late Classic period since to have spread the construction over a somewhat longer period of time, and with a smaller work force, would have extended the continuity of action and the impressiveness of new developments almost indefinitely.

As a practical matter, it is highly doubtful that the rainy season and the accompanying high humidity encountered at most ceremonial centers would have permitted 200 working days each year. Burning and storing the lime cement; quarrying, shaping and hauling stone blocks; and mixing and forming concrete, all of which had to be performed under exposed conditions and with primitive tools and facilities, would not have been possible during wet weather.

(c) *Architectural Adaptation to Available Stone Deposits*

It would be presumptuous to expect that nature would ever favor mankind with the perfect bedded-stone deposit; in fact, it is in its natural qualities that stone finds acceptance and beauty. If one is looking for perfect symmetry and uniform coloration, his order should be placed with a brickmaker rather than the quarrier. And since stone is a product of nature, it should be expected that any given deposit will contain a substantial amount of unusable material. When this factor is coupled with the problems encountered in producing a finished product and the waste thereby created, it can be understood why the better bedded-stone deposits on the Yucatan Peninsula produced no more than about 25% workable stone and 75% rubble stone.

At Uxmal and the other Puuc centers, the stone deposits undoubtedly were the best on the entire Yucatan Peninsula because of the superior quality of the various stone layers and the wide range of thicknesses among those layers. In particular, the Puuc deposits contained a few layers of bedded limestone which were as thin as four to ten inches, and this special feature enabled the architects to have a field day. They were working with the best stone deposits available, and they displayed a remarkable degree of adaptation in adorning their buildings with a riot of designs.

Uxmal and the other nearby Puuc centers, as well as the original, or "old," portion of the construction at Chich'en Itz'a, are all justly famous for the intricate and detailed mosaic designs on the facades of their buildings. This feature is lacking at Tikal, the last, or "new," construction at Chich'en Itz'a, and at Palenque. The use of mosaics was occasioned by the availability of thin layers of limestone rather than because of a revolution in architectural styles. Whenever a different and available building substance presented itself to the Maya, they seized upon the opportunity and made the most of it.

Mosaic designs were created by carefully breaking thin limestone slabs into small rectangular or square cube-shaped stones which could be laid in many patterns utilizing little or no mortar between the pieces. The stones were inserted into the concrete matrix of the exterior wall in the same way that veneer wall stones were installed. On occasion, the exterior wall and the concrete inner core of the building were constructed as a single unit, thus providing for a better bond, but the tendency was to construct the concrete core of the building and then place the veneer and mosaic wall facings (and the necessary back-up concrete portion) against the building core. This latter method created a latent structural defect which in time allowed facing walls to separate from the back-up core and fall to the ground; worse still, the heavier facade, which backed up against the sloping core of the pre-constructed vaults, added the dimension of a heavier mass upon the vertical walls below, thereby exacerbating the problem.

The mosaic effect was precise and distinctive, and shadow and

A portion of the rear facade of the Palace of the Governors, showing the concrete core of the structure (which encased the vaulted rooms) and a mosaic-and-concrete outer section built up against the core.

depth effects, as well as faster installation, were distinct benefits. Architecturally, the mosaic principle was very effective since it allowed for designs, shapes and sizes of patterns on the large building facades which gave a unique balance to the total construction that could not have been achieved by etching shallow indentations into large blocks. The use of smaller mosaic pieces also allowed the architects the luxury of arranging their patterns on the ground before installation.

In passing, it should be noted that the Zapotecs found a deposit of thinly bedded, volcanic-type stone at Mitla, nearly 500 miles away as the crow flies, in a high valley near Oaxaca, and constructed several walls of exquisite, detailed mosaics.

A section of the facade of the west building of the Quadrangle, with elements of a Mexican influence grafted into Maya geometric mosaic patterns.

In addition to the mosaic patterns inserted into the facades of the vertical walls of Maya buildings, we must also take a closer took at the facing blocks which usually constituted the bulk of the exposed portion of the walls of their structures, and here we are able to see how the Maya used concrete to solve what would have otherwise constituted a major structural defect. Although each facing block appears to have been firmly set in its vertical wall, the method of breaking and shaping building blocks at the quarry presented an inherent obstacle to their use. When Earl H. Morris restored the Temple of the Warriors during the late 1920s, he noted that the bed planes of the various stones were rarely at right angles to the faces and, as I have explained the problem, the facing blocks could not be laid course-upon-course in a vertical wall without concrete being placed in the interior cavities which were created by the inward-sloping taper of the stones.

Mosaic facade on the northwest corner of the east building of the Quadrangle.

The vertical walls of most structures, when laid in brick or stone, can either be structurally supportive or simply decorative. A wall which supports the main structure in whole or in part is designated a bearing wall, and it requires each brick or block of stone to be essentially a perfect cube having right-angled corners. This enables the builder to stack the bricks or blocks of stone one-upon-the-other and, either with or without the use of bonding mortar, the wall will rise vertically and will support both itself and additional courses which are added as the wall rises to its desired height. The finished wall will also support the girders upon which a roof or an additional floor can be placed.

Most of the exterior building walls constructed by ancient people prior to Roman times were of the bearing wall type, but the Maya of Late Classic times rarely produced building blocks where the face sides were at right angles to the adjoining sides, and so very little of their

The west building in the Quadrangle, an architectural masterpiece utilizing mosaics.

construction utilized bearing wall stones. They did not have sophisticated tools with which to produce large quantities of building blocks of that type and so they created the veneer method of laying the wall courses on their buildings. This method required the equivalent of a bearing wall to be constructed as each course of stones was laid, and the problem was solved by filling the void behind the face of each stone with a concrete mixture.

A thin layer of mortar is usually found between the exposed edges of facing stones, but behind the joints there can be found the concrete mass which encased the tapered building blocks and produced a solid wall. The net effect of inserting facing blocks into building walls by the veneer method was that their usefulness was mostly ornamental, with structural support being a secondary consideration.

The typical 20th-century residence or office building which uses brick, block or cut stone as a veneer facing often utilizes the alternate, or staggered, placement of each parallel course of material. If we examine a brick wall, it will usually be found that the center of each brick along a given horizontal course will be placed exactly above the mortar joint of each brick on the contiguous lower horizontal course. The foregoing laying method adds some structural strength and stability to the wall, irrespective of whether the wall is designed strictly to serve as a veneer facing or as a bearing wall, since to construct the wall with mortar joints extending in straight, vertical rows encourages cracks along the mortar joints extending up to the full height of the wall. Further, the staggered placement of the bricks provides greater aesthetic appeal in the eyes of many viewers.

The Maya during Late Classic times built nonbearing walls on the veneer principle, but there often existed a conspicuous failure to uniformly stagger the mortar joints between horizontal courses of stones. This has concerned numerous writers because the structural effect of the veneer portion of the wall was somewhat reduced; also, it has been suggested that they overlooked an obvious aesthetic advantage which uniformly staggered mortar joints would have produced.

It must be appreciated that in the process of breaking and sizing facing stones the Maya could not precisely control their shape in the manner which bricks and blocks are produced in today's mass produc-

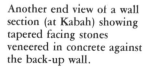
Another end view of a wall section (at Kabah) showing tapered facing stones veneered in concrete against the back-up wall.

tion factories. To produce great quantities of facing stones with identical surface measurements as to both length and width was literally impossible, even though it may have been desirable. Many veneered walls at various ceremonial centers reveal deviations in both horizontal and vertical mortar joint courses across the face of the wall, the reason being tied to the necessity of adapting available facing stones to the job at hand. Had there been an attempt to stagger the mortar joints on a given wall (or group of walls) when construction commenced on a building, the point would have been reached where available facing stones of the desired shape would have been exhausted, requiring other veneered walls in the complex to make-do with a hodgepodge of stone sizes, thus producing crazy-quilt wall patterns.

By the same logic and for the same reasons, it would have been

Side view of a Chac head on the left corner of the second level of the Grand Palace at Sayil.

A portion of the Palace of the Masks at Kabah. Both the front wall and the facade contained row-upon-row of Chac masks having upward-curving noses. Most of the curved noses have broken off over the many years.

equally difficult for the Maya to have built with facing blocks having straight, vertical (i.e., nonstaggered) mortar joints. It is understandable that the limitations of available technology and the nature of the stone at each ceremonial center imposed limitations on construction techniques.

The foregoing furnishes another explanation of the failure to find a standard unit of measurement in Maya construction. They may have developed a measurement system, but it would have provided little assistance in the construction of their stone structures.

Proceeding southeasterly from Uxmal through the Puuc Hills, there can be found the ceremonial centers of Kabah, Sayil and Labna. Although considerably smaller, all of them adopted the same architectural styles found at Uxmal, together with a profusion of mosaic patterns on the facades of their buildings. It is at Kab́ah where we find the most garish and busiest wall to be found anywhere in Maya country, consisting of many Chac masks having long upward-curving noses.

Most of the limestone worked by the Maya, consisting almost entirely of organic ingredients, was not abrasive. Consequently, when somewhat softer layers were encountered, as at Kab́ah, unusual shapes could be created by abrading the stone into various shapes.

But it is Sayil, with its magnificent three-tiered Grand Palace, that is in many ways the most enlightening ceremonial center of the Maya. Its Grand Palace certainly must be considered one of the most beautiful and imposing structures they ever built. One can visualize the rulers, bedecked in ceremonial regalia and accompanied by a retinue of attendants, descending the great central stairway which divides the structure to the cheers of throngs of people assembled in the plaza below. If the Maya ever created a single structure and a setting likely to charge the imagination, this one was their masterpiece.

The Grand Palace is a unique architectural achievement built near the end of the Late Classic era. At most ceremonial centers one encounters buildings constructed upon the remains of older structures, but the great bulk of this edifice was undoubtedly built in a systematic and continuous surge of activity occupying the efforts of possibly 50 workmen during a period of less than 50 years. The available working days during each year would have affected the total construction time frame.

At Sayil the Maya found an excellent medium-sized deposit of bedded limestone very similar in quality to the deposits at Uxmal. It was located on a high mound in the same spot where the Grand Palace is presently located. The Maya examined the stone layers in the deposit very carefully and commenced a unique quarrying and construction program. The key to the project involved controlled quarrying and stone-breaking techniques, together with a maximum utilization of all stone so as to minimize the amount of unusable rubble. They deliberately made advance plans to eliminate the need for a pyramid by incorporating all waste rubble stone into the total structure. In the

Left portion of the Grand Palace at Sayil. The use of round columns and parallel rows of colonnettes on the second level gives this structure the appearance of what we would consider to be a "temple."

process, very little material of any kind was moved more than 300 to 400 feet.

The architects and builders of the Grand Palace made a preliminary investigation of the stone deposit by sample quarrying, and they anticipated the quantities of stone of various sizes and shapes which ultimately would be available for the project. The thick, porous and chert-impregnated layer of between 20 and 25 inches, encountered also at Uxmal, Chich'en Itz'a and Tikal, was pounded and shaped into round columns; the intermediate layers, ranging between 10 and 17 inches, or thereabouts, were broken and shaped for use as wall facing blocks and for steps; and the thinner layers were set aside for making mosaic patterns.

After making a determination of the quantities of stone available

A full view of the Grand Palace at Sayil.

The Great Arch at Labná, an architectural masterpiece utilizing relatively large mosaic pieces.

for various uses, the architects then proceeded to design a palace utilizing to maximum advantage the complete site and all of the available building materials — which consisted almost entirely of stone. The result was an architectural triumph and an object to behold.

The Grand Palace at Sayil was made possible because of a highly skilled group of planners and designers. Unskilled workers could have done most of the manual work, but the project never could have been planned and designed without a nucleus of skilled craftsmen who could be sent to various projects under construction, similar to the pattern followed by the cathedral builders of Europe several hundred years later. They were probably closely associated with the ruling class at a chiefdom level who controlled the political and religious activities of a given geographical area.

For reasons which will be discussed later, it is unlikely that Sayil ever supported a population of any substantial size; in fact, it is generally believed that it was one of the last ceremonial centers to be constructed during the Late Classic era and that it was abandoned soon after being built. Here, as at the other Puuc centers (including Uxmal), there is not the imposing quantity of stelae, glyphs, carvings and other evidence usually associated with rulers-in-residence. This would suggest construction at the Puuc centers was likely seasonal in nature and might have been handled by a work force which could have been deployed and moved from project to project from a distant center of operations.

At Uxmal and Sayil there are found explicit phallic stone objects among the ruins. Some writers have attempted to ascribe religious or art-form significance to them, but any modern quarry operator, supervising a crew of young laborers at a site remote from beer halls and other attractions of community life, would certainly anticipate such expressions of talent from their leisure-time activities. As the old saying goes, "The more things change, the more they seem the same."

PALENQUE and COPÁN

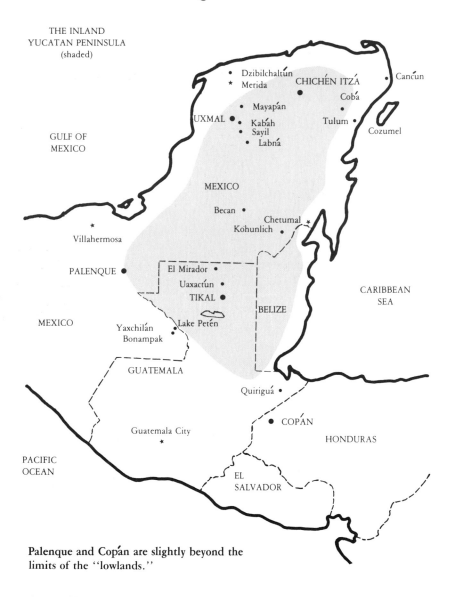

THE INLAND
YUCATAN PENINSULA
(shaded)

• Dzibilchaltún
★ Merida
CHICHÉN ITZÁ
• Cancún

Coba

• Mayapán

UXMAL •
• Kabáh
• Sayil
• Labná

Tulum •

Cozumel

GULF OF
MEXICO

MEXICO

Becan •

Chetumal
Kohunlich •

★
Villahermosa

PALENQUE •
El Mirador •
Uaxactún •
TIKAL •

BELIZE

CARIBBEAN
SEA

MEXICO
Yaxchilán •
Bonampak
Lake Petén

GUATEMALA

Quiriguá • •

• COPÁN

Guatemala City
★

HONDURAS

PACIFIC
OCEAN

EL
SALVADOR

**Palenque and Copán are slightly beyond the
limits of the "lowlands."**

OPPOSITE: Palenque at sunrise.

PALENQUE

Once upon a time there was Palenque.

Situated at the southwesterly edge of the Yucatan Peninsula where the mountains begin to rise above the lowlands, a narrow mountain-canyon plateau encloses a fairyland assortment of ruins known as Palenque. In a lush, tropical setting in the Chiapas rain forest, blessed with a clear, small stream and a view far across the distant lowlands, parrots and macaws with bright plumage and the raucous noises of howler monkeys create a feeling of the unreal. Though somewhat smaller than the other major ceremonial centers, it provides a unique insight into certain aspects of Maya life.

A spot more lovely and idyllic would be difficult to find

anywhere, and in its majestic setting the human spirit would be encouraged to achieve artistic excellence. Indeed, the combination of its secluded, beautiful setting and the stucco artistry on its buildings has set apart Palenque as the gem of Mayadom.

According to archaeologists, most of the structures at Palenque were built between 600-750 A.D. Unlike the veneer wall method of construction utilized so effectively during the Late Classic period at Tikal, Chichén Itzá and Uxmal, the Palenque builders adapted their building techniques to a method which was harmonious with their own available building stone resources.

The limestone deposits found at Palenque were located along the southwesterly edge of the sea which spawned their creation, and they were later raised by the upthrust of the adjoining mountain range. Being formed around the perimeter of the sea, the layers in the Palenque deposits were considerably thinner than those found at the inland sites we have been discussing. As might be expected, those deposits were less uniform in texture and were subjected to a variety of conditions found nearer the seashore during their formative stage. As a result, the limestone at Palenque was generally hard, coarse and subject to irregular cross-fractures as the slabs were pried loose from the deposit. The thinner layers did not have the level, mottled faces of the texture and quality found in the bedding planes of the stone slabs at the major ceremonial sites we have been discussing; rather, on being pried loose during the quarrying operation, most of the stone slabs at Palenque contained irregularities, including "dishes" or small craters often an inch or more in diameter, appearing as pockmarks scattered across both horizontal faces of each slab.

The Maya found they had a stone which was suitable for construction since it could be quarried in layers from bedded deposits, thereby providing the stone masons with reasonably flat slabs. Since most slabs did not have smooth-textured faces, they were broken into pieces and laid flat in walls in the same horizontal position found in the quarries. Fortunately, since the bedded layers varied from as little as two or three inches in thickness to rarely more than ten inches, breaking the thin slabs was a much easier task than that which faced the stone masons at the other ceremonial sites who were required to build with larger and

Slabs of bedded stone at Palenque were generally harder, thinner, unevenly bedded and less susceptible to controlled breaking than the limestone found at the other major Peninsula sites. Chipping and finish trimming of this stone was very difficult.

thicker limestone blocks under the "old" method of construction in vogue prior to Late Classic times.

The method of construction at Palenque therefore must be categorized as an adaptation of the "old" method whereby the bedding planes of the stone slabs were laid horizontal in the walls of the structures.

By using substantial amounts of mortar and thin filler chips, or "chinks," between the layers of stone, wall courses of buildings were laid by placing stones one-upon-the-other in a manner more analogous to a bearing wall arrangement. The exposed exterior stones were veneered in a sense, but their thinner nature allowed them to be

Much of the inner core material in this Palenque building was laid in a horizontal pattern, embedded in concrete and mortar. Exterior walls and interior rooms of all structures were thickly plastered.

embedded into the matrix of the core of the wall, often overlapping each other so as to bond together the entire structure and, in the process, producing a general appearance of evenness to all exposed exterior and interior walls. As might be expected, the use of long, thin slabs of stone, bonded with mortar and concrete, enabled the builders of Palenque to come fairly close to building true corbeled vaults with somewhat less dependence on the monolithic concrete form which was developed to its ultimate at Uxmal and the other Puuc sites.

The utilization of broken slabs of flat-laid stones on exposed building walls naturally left a rough and irregular wall face which was hardly pleasing to the eye. The problem was solved by adorning the walls with thick layers of plaster which could be left white or painted. Not only did the medium of plaster beautify their buildings, it provid-

The exposed end of this wall furnishes an idea of how the various layers of stone actually looked in their natural positions before being quarried. The use of chips as spacers between stones both hastened the laying process and provided a rough edge for holding the plaster covering.

ed an excellent surface for painting scenes of their rulers and religious activities, as well as for glyph writing. Because the available stone lacked the smooth beauty of the layers found in the deposits of the Puuc area, the veneer-type construction which dominated the Late Classic era could not be utilized at Palenque. On the other hand, the thinner stone layers at Palenque had certain advantages, particularly in that faster quarrying and construction was possible. As with the "old" construction method, the builders of Palenque were required to beautify their structures with heavy coats of plaster, a technique which provided both beauty to their structures and other incidental benefits.

On the walls of the portico and central chamber of the Temple of

The Temple of the Sun is an architectural gem. Architectural design at Palenque was unique in that the exterior roof lines of buildings sloped inward, approximately paralleling the angle of the interior vaults.

the Inscriptions can be found over 600 hieroglyphs.

Lacking durable paper and with permanent storage of movable items always presenting a problem, it can be appreciated that the Maya could best advance and develop their skills in painting and writing by having available smooth, plastered walls protected from the elements.

In addition to the several bedded layers of stone in the Palenque deposits which were only a few inches thick, an inspection of exposed portions of the ruins reveals the existence of possibly two thicker layers of stone of good quality and having smooth bedding planes — approximately seven to eight inches and nine to ten inches, respectively. It was from the first-mentioned layer that the large 12½-foot-long rectangular slab was secured for the tomb of the ruler Pacal, which was found within and at the base of the Temple of the Inscriptions.

In 1952, after several years of removing deliberately placed rubble stone from an interior stairway, the excavation crew of Mexican archaeologist Alberto Ruz Lhuillier discovered the Funerary Crypt at the bottom of a vaulted stairway within the Temple of the Inscriptions. A large slab of stone containing a double row of holes was laid across the stairway entrance at the top of the pyramid temple, and it was 80 feet below that there was found proof that the Maya constructed temple pyramids as sepulchral monuments in the manner of the Egyptians.

Evidence abounds that Palenque was a chiefdom and that it reached a fairly high level of civilization, but its remote location in a narrow canyon nearly 1,000 feet above the adjacent lowlands un-

Temple of Inscriptions.

Sculptured stone head of a ruler of Yaxchilán, a Late Classic settlement located on the Usumacinta River approximately 80 miles southeast of Palenque.

Courtyard of the Palace at Palenque.

doubtedly limited its value as a hub of activity for a large population engaged in commerce or farming. The abrupt climb from the lowlands at the base of the mountain in the jungle heat and humidity would have been a deterrent to those coming into the area, even though it must be admitted that difficult terrain was intimately associated with Maya existence.

The ruling nobility possibly lived on-site in or near the palace complex, with the bulk of the supporting population (except for construction workers, servants and lesser administrative officials) living at a distance in the lowlands where they farmed, hunted and traded. The cluster of structures at Palenque is not large, nor is there much flat area. Without its unique and imposing setting, Palenque would have had little to commend it as a location for a seat of government or as a community center.

Was Palenque deliberately located so as to provide a ceremonial center controlled by rulers and priests, or was its setting a coincidence occasioned by another dispensation from nature? The answer is clear since, here again, we find another place where nature laid down surface deposits of bedded limestone, making it possible to construct palaces and temples in the jungle setting.

It might be argued that Palenque was located near or on a trade route between the Chiapas Mountains and the Usumacinta River, and that there was soil in the area which would support farming activities. In addition, a good, small, live stream descended from the mountains, thus providing adequate drinking water. Every condition existed for a reasonable population to locate in the vicinity and to maintain itself for a period of several hundred years. But it should be emphasized that the combination of such conditions would have dictated that the inhabitants select a more logical and available city location — possibly nearer to the present city of Palenque located along the base of the mountains a few miles distant. But history never would have known about the other "Palenque" because there would have been no great ruins to record its existence. Whatever level of civilization the other "Palenque" may have reached would have long since vanished along with the fragile huts which sheltered its inhabitants.

Better stated, the Palenque of the beautiful ruins and the idyllic setting, as we have come to know it, never would have been located exactly where we find it today except for the fortuitous nearby location of bedded-stone deposits. Lacking the so-necessary ingredients for permanent human habitation and survival, it is not surprising that Palenque, too, was eventually abandoned to the jungle.

OPPOSITE: Stela C at Copán.

NOTE: For location map of Copán see pages 4 and 102.

COPÁN

Were it not for unmistakable evidence of similar architectural and construction features, one coming to Copán might wonder whether some foreign people were its builders. Situated near the upper reaches of a small river valley in western Honduras at an altitude of 2,000 feet— barely over the mountain border from Guatemala — Copán neither qualifies as a lowland ceremonial center nor is it geographically a part of the Yucatan Peninsula.

And yet, with its splendid ball court and the so-common features of stone shaping and fitting found elsewhere throughout Maya territory, it was an integral part of the Late Classic Maya era. Like Palenque, Copán was built near the edge of the area we have described as

The Hieroglyphic Stairway at Copán contains the greatest number of
Maya glyphs to be found anywhere.

the lowlands; but it was not surrounded by dense jungle and, unlike
most of the ceremonial centers referred to in this book, Copán was not
constructed of limestone — a very significant feature, as we shall see.

In its own way, Copán is as unique in the Maya picture as is Palenque. The presence of the "corbeled" vault, the use of boot-shaped
vault stones, the bonding of trimmed and shaped building stones with
lime mortar, the existence of numerous stelae, and the worship of common dieties all indicate that Copán maintained an active interchange
of ideas and commerce with other Maya population centers. In fact,
we are told that in 776 A.D. sixteen delegates from various Maya
centers met at Copán to confer with its priests for the purpose of correc-
ting differences in their calendrical reckonings.

If the Maya actually developed a usable system of glyph writing, the center for such activities could have been Copán. The famous Hieroglyphic Stairway has 63 risers, all of which were carved with numerous glyphs — approximately 2,500 in all. The top riser contains full-figure glyphs of the type found at Palenque and Quiriguá. Unfortunately, in the process of restoring the Stairway the numerous glyphs could not be replaced in their original positions, thus making it virtually certain that they will never be deciphered. Time, in its own way, has scrambled the code.

Copán held sway from about 464 A.D. — the date carved on the earliest stela — but the great acropolis and the ornamental sculptures and most of its beautifully carved stelae were constructed between 600 and 800 A.D. during the Late Classic era. And like the other major Maya centers, it appears to have been abandoned sometime after 800 A.D.

The profusion of advanced architectural designs and building features found in the ceremonial centers under discussion suggests the possibility of influences which introduced skills and ideas not indigenous to a people who shared a harsh existence in the jungles and rugged mountains of Mesoamerica. Some writers have argued that Maya temples and palaces simply reflect an architectural projection of the form of their grass and pole huts, but others are not so easily convinced. Unfortunately, we may never develop conclusive evidence, but the possibility of Asian — or even African or European — contacts before and around 500 A.D. cannot be totally discounted.

One of the most intriguing features of Copán is the existence of baroque sculptures created by carvings-in-the-round. On every hand one encounters three-dimensional carvings on stelae, crouching demons guarding the entrances to their temples, and "makara" heads and designs similar to those found in Indonesia. The visages on the stelae and sculptures at Copán suggest the influence of South Asian contacts. The burial custom of placing a piece of jade in the mouth of the deceased, common to the Late Yucatec Maya and the Aztecs, as well as the Chinese, is evident at Copán. It should be noted that the Funerary Crypt of Pacal at Palenque contained a corpse with a jade object placed in his mouth.

This crouching demon, together with a companion, was originally located at the base of the Hieroglyphic Stairway. Similar figures serve as temple guardians in Indonesia.

For years, scholars have debated the possibility that Chinese or other South Asian contacts were had with the Maya of Central America. Some have advanced the unlikely possibility that Chinese ships were "blown" across the broad Pacific, bringing with them additional settlers to add to the existing native population.

On one score there does seem to be a basis for agreement: Most students of the subject believe that the original inhabitants of Mesoamerica were descendants of migrating groups who came across the Bering Straits many thousands of years ago when it constituted a land bridge between Siberia and Alaska. Logically, they gradually worked their way south along land routes, and some of them eventually settled in Mesoamerica. But there is accumulating evidence that by 500 A.D. shipbuilding techniques created craft capable of mastering

Stela A at Copán. The foreign appearance of the facial features of Stela A and Stela C has intrigued scholars for many years.

long and difficult sea routes. If we take a world globe and trace a line across the broad Pacific from, say, Singapore or Saigon to the Pacific Coast of Guatemala, we can determine the approximate distance involved. And it is a great distance, across a broad and forbidding ocean following a route close to the equator. The chances of such an ocean voyage being survived by even a minimal number of people at that date would have been practically nil.

On the other hand, if we start at the same point and follow a route in a northeasterly direction past the Phillipine Islands and along the east coast of Japan to a point south of the Aleutian Islands, thence across the northern Pacific Ocean to the west coast of Alaska or Canada, and thence south along the coast of California and Mexico, we can determine that the total distance involved is almost exactly the same as if the journey were to have been made straight across the Pacific. An

The Ball Court at Copán.

ocean voyage following the route just indicated never would have been far from land, and it would have picked up the easterly flowing Japanese current and the westerly winds which would have moved the craft toward the Canadian coast. Upon reaching the west coast of North America, the California current would have hastened the ship and its passengers southerly along the shoreline of California and Mexico.

If Mesoamerica received its original population from Asia, it would seem quite natural that subsequent seaborne voyagers from South Asia would have preferred to travel a route as near to land as possible so as to be able to go ashore periodically to secure food and fresh water. And, since ancient people found the sea to be their best highway, coming down the west coast of North America by boat would have been easier than traveling southward from Alaska by foot over difficult terrain.

The possibility of South Asian contacts by boat before or during the Late Classic era cannot be dismissed out of hand. Recent discoveries off the west coast of California reported by Dr. James Robert Moriarity of the University of San Diego point to the possibility that Chinese ships may have traversed Pacific coastal waters in that area in the distant past. Ship anchors and other stone relics have been found and recovered, their geology suggesting that they only could have come from quarries in South China. Further, Chinese writings dating from about 600 A.D. refer to distant voyages to the land "Fusang," believed to be the Chinese name for ancient Mexico.

If in fact there were contacts by sea from South Asia, Africa or the Mediterranean long before Columbus arrived, wind and water currents probably made it unlikely that many ocean craft ever returned to their home ports. The long return voyage, with its toll on human endurance and the existence of adverse winds and ocean currents, would have discouraged many seafarers from trying to return to the land whence they came. Also, the same problems, coupled with the risks and the great amount of time involved, almost certainly ruled out any possibility of two-way commerce. Perhaps the real significance of the "discovery" made by Columbus was the fact that his was a recorded round-trip journey legitimized in perpetuity by reason of being fostered by the Spanish Crown.

Any pre-Columbian ocean voyages bringing people to Mesoamerica undoubtedly would have been in ships containing sufficient provisions to maintain the lives of those aboard and having necessary tools and equipment adequate to accommodate the ships' needs and the objectives of the journey. Certainly, it would be naive in the extreme to visualize a Noah's Ark, with plants, seeds, horses, cows, pigs and other manner of personal property generally associated with colonization efforts. Thus, we find that the Maya domesticated different animals from those found in South Asia, Africa or Europe, they developed and subsisted upon different food crops, and they did not develop the technology whereby they could make metal tools. Except for claimed traces of pottery which might have been brought from Asia, it would appear reasonably safe to conclude that any sporadic contacts from South Asia, Africa or the Mediterranean would have introduced limited numbers of people who brought with them basic

Olmec head from LaVenta, now to be seen in a large park at Villahermosa. Similar heads and other indications suggest that the Olmec culture (which predated the Maya) could have been influenced by ocean voyagers from Africa or South Asia.

skills in the arts and crafts, as well as religious beliefs, which could have affected their architecture and their living habits and customs.

If the unusual baroque sculpture at Copán tells us something of Maya society, why do we not find an equal abundance of similar features at other major ceremonial centers? The clear answer is that the Maya at Copán were working with a different type of building stone. As has been mentioned, the hard limestone found at most places on the Yucatan Peninsula did not lend itself readily to carvings-in-the-round. After the stone layers were separated from their beds, the typical limestone could be cut and carved to a depth of approximately one inch in the area of the bedding planes of each stone, but to produce carvings much deeper was a difficult task because the hard limestone was more than a match for available stone-cutting tools. Occasionally, a soft limestone was found, such as that which produced the Chac masks and noses at Kab'ah, but that situation was the exception; even then, the use of mosaics and cutting the nose shapes with rawhide and abrasives was a simpler process than gouging and carving intricate recessed and rounded shapes and forms into the limestone with stone tools.

We have previously mentioned that volcanic materials, such as pozzolan and tuff, sometimes contain cementitious qualities when blown from craters and disbursed across the landscape. At Cop'an, an extremely unusual deposit of volcanic tuff, intermixed with a clayey material which formed a greyish-green substance sometimes referred to as a "trachyte," was found. The stone was relatively soft when quarried, but it hardened to a brick-like texture after being exposed to the air for a reasonable time. In addition, the unusual deposit contained thick bedded layers with stone which could be separated into large chunks the size of stelae, as well as thinner layers from which were produced facing blocks for the walls of pyramids and buildings and for stairway steps.

Because the Cop'an trachyte was initially soft enough to be worked, the stone masons and sculptors used greenstones and other cutting devices, such as bone or horns, and they were able to create detailed and elaborate carvings. It took but a short time for the volcanic tuff to form a chemical outer layer of temperature-and-weather-resistant hardness. I have had personal experience with a very similar material, and the resistance created after some tuffaceous stones are shaped and then exposed to the air and elements for a short time is amazing. However, as indicated, such deposits are rare and are found where volcanic activity existed in the distant past.

The immediate vicinity surrounding Cop'an in the narrow river valley supported several small settlements, but its relative isolation and limited life-sustaining land and forest area gave little reason for its continued existence after its stone deposit had been quarried and utilized.

COBÁ, TULUM, MAYAPÁN and DZIBILCHALTÚN
(Northern Yucatan)

THE INLAND
YUCATAN PENINSULA
(shaded)

Dzibilchaltún
Merida
CHICHÉN ITZÁ
Cancún
Cobá
Mayapán
UXMAL
Kabáh
Sayil
Labná
Tulum
Cozumel

GULF OF
MEXICO

MEXICO

Becan
Chetumal
Köhunlich

Villahermosa

PALENQUE

El Mirador
Uaxactún
TIKAL

BELIZE

CARIBBEAN
SEA

MEXICO

Yaxchilán
Bonampak
Lake Petén

GUATEMALA

Quiriguá

COPÁN

Guatemala City

HONDURAS

PACIFIC
OCEAN

EL
SALVADOR

OPPOSITE: The huge Pyramid of Nohuch Mul rises above the jungle at Cobá.

LESSER CITIES AND
CEREMONIAL CENTERS

Although our discussion has been focused on the five most-prominent ceremonial centers built by the Maya, it would be inappropriate and lacking in direction to consider them in isolation. Space does not permit an evaluation of the great number of ruins left by the Maya nor, for that matter, would such an attempt necessarily yield answers proportional to the effort expended. On the other hand, it would appear helpful to draw some comparisons with lesser-known cities and ceremonial centers in those areas of study which are pertinent to the theme of our discussion.

A preliminary view of the large ceremonial centers being analyzed, considered in connection with smaller ceremonial centers which have been restored and hundreds of unrestored ruins, would seem to indicate that the former probably would have been the religious and political centers from which their influence spread to numerous satellite communities. It might be assumed that Chich́en Itźa, Uxmal and Tikal were the civic and ceremonial centers of the Late Classic era in their respective geographical regions, and it would also seem that such communities as Mayaṕan, Dzibilchaltún and Cob́a — to cite a few of many examples — were definitely inferior settlements. This assessment appears to follow because the quality and quantity of the stone structures found at the last three sites were substantially inferior to those of the larger centers.

Various archaeologists have commented adversely on the stone-work at Mayaṕan, Dzibilchaltún, Cob́a and Tulum (a Post Classic settlement), classifying their stone-work (and, by implication, the sites themselves) as poor, crude, inferior and decadent. An inspection of the structures at those sites leaves no doubt that they lack the quality and beauty of the stone-work at Tikal, Chich́en Itźa, Uxmal and other Puuc sites. However, if our analysis of the building stone available to the Maya at different locations has validity, the relative importance of at least some of the major ceremonial centers featured in this book would appear suspect.

A comparison of the five most-notable ceremonial centers with many smaller settlements once again emphasizes a disturbing contradiction: The large ceremonial centers with the most-elaborate and impressive structures are found in areas which were least conducive to human occupation; the somewhat smaller sites which have poor quality stone-work and inferior structures are often found at sites where conditions for human habitation were definitely more favorable.

Mayaṕan, the walled city, sustained a substantial population into Post Classic times. Its location was unique because it had numerous cenotes from which its inhabitants were able to secure year-round water. Dzibilchaltún, located a short distance north of present-day Merida, supported a small population continuously from about 800 B.C. to approximately 1,000 A.D.; it, too, had access to a large, open and readily available cenote and circulating underground water sources

Temple of the Seven Dolls at Dzibilchaltún. It was constructed of rough stone and concrete.

which existed close to the ground surface. Cobá, located approximately 30 miles inland from the Caribbean Sea, was nestled amidst four small lakes which served its inhabitants in various ways. Each of these sites had generally better soil and a less rugged terrain than Tikal, Uxmal or, for that matter, Chich'en Itzá; further, and of considerable importance, the inhabitants of Chich'en Itzá, Tikal and Uxmal had to secure their water from deep cenotes, distant aguadas or from artificial on-site storage reservoirs. Continuous habitation at Cobá and Mayapán, as well as at Dzibilchaltún, over a period of many centuries has been documented by archaeologists.

Can we logically maintain that Cobá, as an example, was an inferior city or ceremonial center as compared to Uxmal or Chich'en Itzá? Not necessarily; in fact, just the opposite could have been the case.

Tourists by the thousands come from nearby Cancún to visit the Post Classic ruins at Tulum. Perched on a bluff overlooking the Caribbean Sea, the Spaniards compared it to their grand city of Seville.

From an examination of the stone-work at Cobá, it appears that the populace probably extended itself to construct several large pyramids and other structures containing stone-work much inferior to that found at Tikal, Uxmal and Chichén Itzá. Architectural decorations reflected in stone incising and sculpturing are extremely rare, and we find that stucco plaster was the main decorative medium — as was the case at Tulum, Kohunlich and other east coast sites. This group of communities — and they were in fact probably minor population centers — constructed their pyramids and temples of surface caprock found at each respective location.

But when we compare the environmental advantages of Cobá, for instance, with Uxmal and the other Puuc sites, and even Tikal and Chichén Itzá, the likelihood of an established population having existed over a period of many years is much greater, and more evident, at Cobá. Cobá was the hub for a network of roads (*sacbes*) which radiated out in several directions towards other population centers (which, incidentally, did not include Chichén Itzá).

Why, then, do we find such poor stone-work at the locations we have been using for comparison? Were their inhabitants shiftless, lazy and untalented, or was there another reason? When I was in Cobá in January, 1979, the question hit me full force; and it was several months later — after I made the discovery on January 30th at Chichén Itzá that the answer lay in the fact that some areas did not have access to good bedded building stone — that Jack Decker began a search to determine why someone had not delved into the matter in view of the existence of obvious unexplained discrepancies.

His search of published reports revealed that the same question troubled J. Eric Thompson, who has been previously quoted as suggesting that a geologist should examine the stone deposits at the various centers. Thompson was unable to discover the real reason why the stone-work at Cobá was so inferior, but he did come close to the general answer, as noted in his 1932 publication:

> . . . Indeed, it is remarkable that the typical features of northwest Yucatan 'Renaissance' architecture should be so conspicuously absent (at Cobá). There are a number of possible explanations of this. Cobá may have been uninhabited during the height of this period, contact (with other northwest Yucatan sites) may not have existed, or the relationships may not be apparent for geological reasons. It would be interesting for a geologist to make a survey of the structural possibilities of the limestone encountered in different parts of the Maya area   The hard crystalline limestone found in the Toledo region of southern British Honduras, for example, is probably the cause of the excellency of the masonry at Lubaantun. Copán was similarly blessed with an excellent stone of a tuffaceous nature which is particularly adaptable for shaping into square or oblong stones, or for sculpturing in the semi-round. The boot-shaped vaulting stone occurs at Copán, and again in northwest Yucatan, where it is

associated with well-squared veneer stone and stone sculpture which approaches the round. Are these associations fortuitous, the results of culture contacts, or due to the nature of the stone employed? The writer believes that the regional differences in architecture and the employment of worked stone largely depended on the nature of the building stone at hand. In the Peten and Coba region this appears to be of poor quality. Until this possibility is negatived by geologists we shall not be in a position to state that Northwest Yucatan was not in a position to influence Coba architecturally.

Unfortunately, neither Thompson nor those who followed in his path pursued the matter; if they did, none was able to provide the correct answer. Thompson's sixth sense anticipated the answer, but his thoughts and suggestions were ignored. The contributions to archaelogy made by that eminent Mayanist would surely have been expanded if the solution had been made available to him.

In his 1978 Handbook on *"Tikal"*, William R. Coe mentions that Early Classic masonry construction (about 550 A.D.) was distinct from that of Late Classic times. He states that monuments of the earlier period were made of limestone having flint-like characteristics, whereas Late Classic monuments were distinguished by "marked bedding planes." The last observation is significant in that it is one of the few references I have been able to find recognizing the existence of bedding planes as they might affect monuments — such as stelae, altar stones or other structures. It has also been observed by others, in addition to the comment made by J. Eric Thompson, that the structures located at Lubaantun in what is now the southern portion of Belize may have been located where they were because of a nearby deposit containing "lenses" of bedded limestone.

The last layer of limestone formed in that ancient sea was coarser, less uniform in quality and less dense than earlier layers, as well as being quite thick. Any quarrying activity would have naturally taken that layer from the top of the deposit and subjected it to use as early as, if not prior to, the lower layers. Thus, the numerous large stelae and round altar stones (several of which I measured at approximately 25 inches in thickness) of Early Classic times probably came from that stone layer.

Coe also stated that stelae constructed during Late Classic times were not carved on their rear surfaces, which possibly suggests that the particular stone layer (also about 25 inches thick, but which contained a 6-inch and a 19-inch layer divided by a very fine and indistinguishable seam line) might have had a deep-pitted bedding plane on one side which discouraged any attempts at carving.

The cumulative effect of the body of knowledge contributed by the many writers, explorers, archaeologists and other students of the Maya, including those cited in this work, has provided valuable background and tie-in assistance. It is indeed unfortunate that in years past certain writers advanced the unsupportable premises that the Yucatan Peninsula *contained inexhaustible quantities of easily cut building stone* and that the Maya accepted the drudgery of *pecking* smooth faces upon their facing stones. The latter group unwittingly diverted all future investigations of Maya stone-work and certain other relevant aspects of Maya life into a dead-end road.

It is entirely possible — and even quite probable — that various Maya settlements which built with inferior surface caprock adorned with plaster, or those settlements which in fact had no limestone rock available for building purposes, may have been centers of influence of greater importance than some of the five major ceremonial centers featured in this book. Many seacoast and river valley areas provided available year-round culinary (and sometimes irrigation) water, tillable land, commercial and trading contacts, and superior food sources. In the context of the comparisons we have been making, it would appear that the importance of the five featured ceremonial sites must be found in their religious (or combined religious-political) importance of the times.

It is significant that at Cobá and Mayapán, as well as at other locations, the Maya gathered surface caprocks in the vicinity, packed them a considerable distance, and stacked them in pyramids in a massive community effort. The religious import of the truncated pyramid, with its temple structure on top, cannot be disregarded even though, as previously explained, the pyramid also may have been a waste dump for a stone-quarrying operation. The huge pyramid of Nohuch Mul at Cobá, built entirely of shapeless caprock and adorned with painted plaster, is adequate proof that pyramids existed as abodes for their gods. Pyramids could have had no utility except for religious purposes, and their sizes and numbers at places such as Cobá are testimonials to the religious fervor of the times. Whatever the reason or reasons, the amount of stone construction at Cobá, as well as at Dzibilchaltún and Mayapán, was also greatest during the Late Classic surge of building activity.

The pyramids of the Maya had much in common with the great cathedrals of Europe which were built a few hundred years later.

We find the limestone at Cobá to be basically identical in hardness, texture and composition with that found at Tikal, Uxmal and Chichén Itzá. From every possible analysis of conditions existing at all four sites, it can only be concluded that the lack of smooth-faced building stone at Cobá was due to the total, or near total, absence of bedded-stone deposits from which there could have been secured natural, smooth surfaces from horizontal layers. It is therefore easy to understand why Cobá, Kohunlich, the Post Classic settlement of Tulum, and numerous other Maya cities and ceremonial centers — including even Palenque — adorned their important structures with smooth plaster.

New plant life takes over a Cob'a field soon after the jungle is cut and burned.

AGRICULTURE IN A JUNGLE SETTING

It is a challenge of substantial magnitude to devote a single page to any discussion of the Maya without inserting a passing commentary relating to the harsh and forbidding environment everywhere apparent at most inland locations. Poor or nonexistent soil, a general lack of drinking water, uncertain and often insufficient rainfall for crops, a rough and rocky terrain, and the presence of a pervasive jungle growth would have added up to nothing but trouble during Late Classic times. Any one of the enumerated conditions, standing alone, would have been a major deterrent to human colonization, but taken in total there existed a combination of problems which would have allowed for marginal subsistence under the best of circumstances.

On several occasions, I have traveled the land route from Chich'en Itz'a west to Merida, and thence south to Uxmal, approximately 120 miles, and in the entire distance there is not an observable live stream or spring. As for tillable land within view of the highway, very few fields contain soil of sufficient depth to accommodate a plow without risk of damage from large rocks. Except for a dozen or so small settlements on either side of Merida, limestone rock and a growth of jungle brush and trees constitutes the main source of scenery. The same scene, subject only to localized variations, exists across all of the inland Yucatan Peninsula. The poverty of the earth is everywhere apparent.

The Maya built plaster-lined chultuns (rainwater storage cisterns), both surface and underground types, in the plazas and around the buildings in their ceremonial centers; and, where the terrain was suitable, they also constructed leak-proof, clay-bottomed aguadas (ponds) to store rain and surface drainage waters. The chultuns had limited capacities and the aguadas had problems — the waters would have become tepid and slimy, and there would have been competition from thirsty snakes, rodents, birds and other wildlife, not to mention local dogs. I can personally attest to the anxiety experienced when it becomes necessary to share a water hole with a big, thirsty and hot, diamond-back rattler in an ugly mood.

The artificial water sources probably sustained basic domestic needs for reasonable periods of time when severe shortages of rainfall periodically troubled the Peninsula; but, over the long run, the lack of rainfall had a permanent and severe effect on the food-support system of any given community. Long periods without rainfall would have caused maize to wilt and become stunted, and even die, and there would have been similar adverse effects on all other plant and animal life, both in the jungle and in cultivated plots around the countryside. Most areas of the inland northern Yucatan Peninsula and the central Petén area of the Peninsula lying north of Tikal always were on the frontier of human habitation. The dilemma which constantly presents itself is that justification for large settlements in the region was absent before Late Classic times. The food-support system of the Maya across most of the inland Yucatan Peninsula never did, nor does it now, add up to a favorable situation.

The inland Peninsula then, as now, was subject to extreme climatic variations where "average" rainfall conditions would be meaningless because in some years the dry season might be very short, while in other years the dry season might constitute the only season. Devastating hurricanes have periodically ravaged most of the Peninsula, uprooting large trees and spreading massive destruction in their paths. Climatic conditions in so-called "normal" seasons also have experienced extreme variations from area to area. In sum, the likelihood of favorable weather conditions being present when critically needed to assist the thin veneer of unproductive soil in producing maize or other crops usually involved poor odds.

Food sources dependent on the ecologically fragile flora and fauna of the jungle, supplemented by agricultural activities tied to the vagaries of rainfall and other weather conditions, cannot be properly analyzed by separately studying each of the various factors entering into the picture. Food production is a composite of many variables where the failure of a single, critical component can result in a total crop failure. Isolated studies of soil types, rainfall, crop varieties, planting and harvesting methods, and similar contributing factors are really of little help in determining the agricultural potential of a given area, except to emphasize the problems inherent in each isolated area of study. The problem in determining the agricultural potential of the Maya was magnified by the limitations imposed upon agricultural pursuits by reason of the absence of simple metal tools, such as plows, shovels and hoes. The component elements essential to the production of agricultural crops are not equally weighted, and it is essential that each be properly diagrammed and allotted its proper degree of importance in order that an experienced opinion can be expressed. None of the writings I have encountered has met the foregoing criteria.

(a) Slash-and-Burn Farming

Modern Maya utilize slash-and-burn farming practices, and we know that the same procedures were followed in ancient times. The method is essentially similar in many respects to the fallow system of dry farming wheat land in use today, except that the burning process permitted the residue from each crop to be disposed of rather easily by people who lacked mechanical equipment for removing or plowing under such material. Burning also tended to kill or retard the growth of plants which were undesirable, and it consumed many of their seeds.

When an agricultural area had been fully cleared and devoted to crop farming, it was found that the slash-and-burn method would permit cropping a plot of land (called a *milpa*) for several years before crop production seriously declined because of depleted soil conditions. Since much of the inland Yucatan Peninsula could be classified as jungle, the soils were constantly leached by rainfall, and it was necessary for the milpas to lie fallow for several years before they were again returned to agricultural production. Run-down soils of the type found in jungles or other areas where heavy rainfall contributes to a rank growth of vegetation are notorious for the low protein content of their crops.

For more than 50 years I have been involved in the production and harvesting of corn (maize), wheat, oats, barley, potatoes and other vegetables, alfalfa, and numerous types of grasses and other livestock feed and forage crops produced from lands in the arid western portion of the United States which have been wrested from desert sagebrush and mountain forests. I can personally bear witness to having observed the rapid decline of fertile, virgin soils from productive to marginal uses in that short time span.

Slash-and-burn land clearing practices in areas where virgin soil was originally devoted to grass was one thing; applying the method to jungle forests was definitely something else. Modern equipment makes it possible to uproot and remove large trees from forested areas with very little manpower; and in those areas containing sagebrush or small trees, large crawler tractors with heavy rails or massive chains can accomplish the same job with ease. The Maya, on the other hand, found it necessary to "girdle" each tree by cutting around the trunk through the layer of bark so as to prohibit further growth. After the trees had died and dried, the forest area would have been fired, and the resulting conflagration would have consumed the dry material in its path.

Implicit in the concept of slash-and-burn agriculture is the expectation that most of the crop residue be cut and placed at or near ground level so that burning will effectively consume everything; but this is not so easily accomplished in the jungle forest. We know that forest fires leave large amounts of dead, blackened stumps and remnants of trees which fast-moving fires never completely consume. For the Maya to have prepared such areas for cropping — assuming they were overlaid with good soil — would have necessitated the removal of most or all of the standing residue, which consisted in large measure of large stumps, as well as the root systems which would not have burned and in a short time would have proved to be very much alive. Lacking metal shovels, hoes and grubbing axes, the work of the Maya subsequent to burning the forest would have just begun. In short, it often would have bordered on the impossible.

The Maya planted maize by using a fire-hardened, pointed stick which they pushed into the ground so that a few kernels could be placed in the hole. Similarly, fire-hardened stumps and tree remnants from slash-and-burn fires would have remained, if no further treatment had been applied, for many years before they would have decayed and become soil humus. In fact, the firing process in many cases actually would have created more detrimental effects than benefits.

Nor should it be expected that an area left unattended after a slash-and-burn firing would have adopted a benign status during the many years it would have required for tree trunks, roots and stumps to rot away. Nature has its own processes, and they do not necessarily follow the path man might wish. Burning rarely would have killed all tree growth, and after ensuing rains, new, tough shoots would have appeared for the purpose of rejuvenating the forest. In those rare instances where root growth might have been killed, the Maya would have encountered another unexpected problem — as I have found to be the case from first-hand experience clearing forest lands — in that the virgin soil almost always would have been taken over by noxious weeds and vines, such as the ever present morning glory (*xail*) found in the Maya jungle.

In the milpas that had been farmed for several years and where

A better-than-average crop of maize was harvested from this small, rocky plot located between Merida and Uxmal.

soil fertility had seriously declined, similar weeds and vines would have proliferated and strangled the pitiful patches of maize struggling for existence.

The ability of the modern farmer to change the natural habitat has depended upon metal tools, power-driven machinery, insecticides, sprays, fertilizers, genetically selected crops and crop-rotation practices. Notwithstanding such means, I have seen soils which were taken from once-rich sagebrush and forest lands subjected to erosion, inadequate fertilization, infestations of perennial noxious weeds, and otherwise abused to the point where crop yields were insufficient to justify the labor and expenses involved. In such cases, the better part of wisdom has been to return those lands to more nearly their natural, original condition, if possible.

We can be certain that the Maya experienced the enumerated problems in their attempts to convert the jungle to farmland. They were hopelessly out-manned by the ordinary forces of nature in most of the jungle portion of the Yucatan Peninsula, leaving them scant opportunity of creating an agricultural base. We can be certain that, in those isolated instances where they may have partially succeeded, their success was shortlived and they found that nature could only be pushed aside so far before retaliation occurred. The Maya certainly were aware that there was a limit to which man could impose his will upon nature.

(b) Survival in a Total Jungle Environment

Any effort to understand the Maya and their involvement with the mass of limestone which was constantly underfoot would be totally inadequate without considering the counterpart of their existence — the jungle: awesome, mysterious, forbidding. The dense growth of vines, shrubs and trees has effectively hidden its secrets from all who have looked into its invisible depths. It has relentlessly struggled for survival in the shallow, infertile soil lying in pockets across the face of the land, sending down roots which have clawed their way into every crevice and crack in that great expanse of limestone.

Yet, despite the poverty of the earth to which it is attached, the jungle has survived and thrived by adapting to the warm climate and drawing strength from heavy seasonal rains. Even during the dry season, a considerable amount of moisture needed for survival is furnished by humid breezes coursing across the Peninsula.

The perpetual presence of the jungle and its ability to rejuvenate itself has defied all attempts to properly understand the land and its history. Its entangling growth has effectively hidden the geology of much of the Yucatan Peninsula, together with much of the history of the people who have inhabited the area. The jungle is everywhere; its immensity has intimidated all who have studied the Maya and their culture, so much so that there has never been a better example of the old adage that one cannot see the forest for the trees.

A closer look into the jungle will, however, provide a clearer picture of its true nature. To the Maya the jungle provided many of the necessities of life: various fruits, berries, seeds, honey, papaya, avocado, ramon nuts, turkeys, rabbits, quail, possums, deer, a variety of birds, insects, peccaries, iguanas, snakes, rodents, miscellaneous crawling things and, in swampy areas, fish, turtles and other aquatic animals.

It is generally believed that ramon nuts furnished an important ingredient in the Maya diet. While the meat portion of the nut may not have an appealing taste to a 20th-century reader, it must be observed that, within reason, tastes can be acquired from necessity and that many ancient peoples derived a substantial portion of their living from very mundane natural sources, such as pith of trees, nuts, seeds, grasses, roots, and the like.

In a total jungle environment it was quite possible for a population of a given size to exist and maintain itself. The main problem associated with jungle life was that a people who relied primarily on hunting could not substantially enlarge their numbers, with increasing demands upon food supply sources, except at the risk of upsetting the fragile ecological balance of nature and suffering eventual starvation or having to move from place to place in order to secure food.

To what extent did the Maya really supplement their jungle existence by agricultural pursuits? We know they produced squash, beans, root crops (such as "manioc" [which produces tapioca] and a variety of sweet potato) and, most important of all, maize (corn). Their obsession with maize permeated their very existence; it was literally an object of worship to them. Their ability to produce maize has been the cornerstone of most investigations into the agricultural base of their existence.

We have just discussed the severe limitations of slash-and-burn agriculture in a jungle setting. Further, almost everywhere across the inland Yucatan Peninsula one finds such shallow and infertile deposits of soil as to discourage any farming activity, a condition aptly described by the Spanish Bishop Diego de Landa who, writing in the mid-1500s, characterized the country as having ". . .the least amount of earth I have ever seen."

To the extent that farming pursuits may have been imposed on the jungle environment, the necessity of moving to new milpas every few years certainly interfered with the ecosystem of the jungle, particularly in that the competition for space adversely affected the natural home of wild animals. It is doubtful that the trade-off, to the extent that it actually occurred, compensated for the loss sustained as a result of encroachments on the jungle. Although pursued diligently, the production of maize around the five large ceremonial centers was probably very limited at best, there being no real comparison between conditions on the Yucatan Peninsula and those which prevailed in the fertile valleys of Oaxaca and Tehuacán where maize was developed and nurtured for several thousand years.

(c) *Technological Interference with the Ecosystem*

Referring again to the method by which the Maya made cement from open-air kilns using green firewood, that practice may have created a situation which could have had a far-reaching impact on the ecology of a given area. Construction of the large ceremonial centers required substantial amounts of lime cement for making concrete, mortar and plaster, and the Maya must have been required to travel far afield in search of green firewood and suitable limestone sources found in combination. Green firewood would have been cut and carried to a common burning area within a radius of not more than about a half mile, but beyond that distance it probably was more practical to secure green trees and burn the limestone farther away inasmuch as the lime cement produced by that method was more dense and easier to haul, and the process was less wasteful, than attempting to transport the firewood and unburned limestone to the ceremonial centers being constructed.

The effect of such selective clear-cutting of large areas of forest for cement-making purposes may have tended to reduce dependency on slash-and-burn practices as a means of providing agricultural lands where the forest and good soil happened to coincide, but the problem of eradicating the remaining stumps and root systems constantly remained. Furthermore, that type of clear-cutting would have been highly selective for the reason that jungle vines and similar growth did not lend themselves to proper burning. The net result of the foregoing practice around the large ceremonial centers could have resulted in such an ecological imbalance as to require the importation of food from less-affected areas for extended periods of time. Importing food, to the extent it may have been necessary, would have created administrative problems and a burden upon other producing areas of such magnitude as to give that endeavor a life of short duration.

． ．

It is now possible to visit the major ruins of the Peninsula by means of a paved road system, where one can observe the countryside and existing ways of life and then make mental comparisons to the situation in Late Classic times. Many communities can now exist by virtue of the deep-well pump, which can raise water from the water table underlying many feet of limestone; but the Maya were forced to rely upon available cenotes, undependable aguadas and limited artificial means of storing water during the dry season. The modern Maya can clear thorny bushes, shrubs, vines and small trees from their trails with the machete, which is universally used everywhere throughout Central and South America; but their ancestors did not have access to any tool remotely approaching its versatility. As for plant foods, the orange and the prolific banana were imported by the Spaniards; the native manioc plant (which produces a root having a taste similar to a cross between a potato and a parsnip) was the nearest substitute to the modern potato. The Late Classic Maya domesticated and ate dogs and turkeys, but they had no large meat-producing animals, such as beef, bison and horses; the small native deer, while plentiful, in its dressed-out condition would have failed to produce 50 pounds of food, hide and other by-products. The turkey was domesticated, but its output of meat and eggs made it a poor competitor to that great universal food machine: the chicken.

The Maya had a hard row to hoe, and it can only be concluded that farming pursuits generally ran a distant second to that of the hunter in the jungles of the inland Yucatan Peninsula during the Late Classic era.

The "Palace" at Palenque: A ruler's residence or a temple?

THE LARGE CEREMONIAL
CENTERS AS "CITIES"

Any in-depth study of the Maya must sooner or later grapple with the question of whether the five great stone complexes were cities or whether they served a different role in their lives. It has been argued that they were true cities serving as centers for large on-site and surrounding populations; on the other hand, a contrary school of thought contends that they were essentially ceremonial centers serving combined religious-governmental purposes and as market places for populations much smaller than their physical sizes might suggest.

In preceding chapters we noted that the five large ceremonial centers were generally located where farming and other food-producing sources were tenuous at best. Coupled with that fact is the further disturbing dilemma that, as previously noted, the apparently smaller and obviously inferior ceremonial centers were located where food and water sources, as well as general living conditions, were decidedly superior.

The natural inclination of anyone looking at the large ceremonial centers is to equate their sizes with substantial urban-type populations. That approach must necessarily be premised on the assumption that the Maya were building structures commensurate with the size and needs of a given population. It also must be assumed that the population would have located at the particular site by choice, that the means of providing food, water and shelter were reasonably adequate, and that the remains of the structures being examined furnish reasonable evidence of having been used by a resident population at the time and place under consideration. If any one of the foregoing assumptions is seriously flawed, it then becomes necessary to look for other explanations.

The difficulty with any analysis of population numbers at the large ceremonial centers we have been discussing is that stereotyped approaches don't work. We are left with mysteries — why were the "cities" originally established where we find them, were they really "cities," what size populations did they support, and why were they all abandoned to the jungle by 900 A.D.?

History tells us that most large cities have prospered at sites where fertile lands produced agricultural surpluses or where there were major trade routes, such as river waterways or seaports. None of the five major ceremonial centers could have qualified under the foregoing criteria, or for other reasons, as a location where numerous people would choose to live for extended periods of time. Nor is there sufficient evidence available in the form of substantial quantities of the debris of human habitation to furnish convincing proof of a large population in the inland Yucatan Peninsula during Late Classic times. The general consensus of opinion is coming around to the conclusion that the large ceremonial centers of the Maya were not in fact cities and that they probably served community functions to a limited extent.

In striking contrast to the precise arrangement of geometric designs and the profuse adornment found on the facades of many Maya buildings, it has long been recognized that at nearly all ceremonial centers there is lacking any logical placement of structures in a city lay-out pattern. Their haphazard locations often would not qualify, for that matter, as being designed to accommodate a ceremonial center. The intermixture of palaces, pyramid temples, ball courts and other structures, often being placed at oblique angles in relation to each other, presents a rude departure from the harmonious designs and architectural balance typical of the various buildings in a particular complex.

The explanation, of course, is that the various structures were located where the problems of quarrying the bedded-stone deposits, finding a building site with a solid base, and removing waste and broken stone to a pyramid location could all be best overcome with the expenditure of the least amount of labor.

Although the Great Plaza at Tikal appears to have one of the best arrangements of pyramids and palaces for community use, the simple fact remains that to remove the large deposit of bedded stone which once reposed in what is now the open plaza area left little choice for the positioning of those edifices other than at the perimeter locations where they are found.

(a) The Real Significance of Vaulted Rooms

A logical approach to the problem of whether the ceremonial centers were cities would dictate that, among other things, an analysis should be made of those structures, usually referred to as palaces, where there can be found enclosed rooms, since by the standards applied by most temperate-zone readers, rooms are often equated with living quarters. But we are not just dealing with rooms: We are vitally concerned with *vaulted rooms* — a feature of Maya construction which persisted for at least 1,000 years.

And it would seem that a determination should be made as to whether the vaulted rooms generally served as palace-type living quarters for Maya rulers or whether their function, like the pyramids,

End-section of a 60-foot-long vaulted room build across the front of the Temple of the Warriors by the Toltec-Maya at Chichén Itzá. The connecting capstone at the top of the vault is 28 feet above floor level.

was basically similar to that of a typical religious temple.

In an earlier chapter we learned that constructing the vaulted portion of palace and other rooms was greatly simplified by the use of concrete, whereby thrust forces were neutralized and overcome by making the vault a part of a monolithic unit. What had theretofore been a structure very difficult to build and extremely limited in area instantly became so standardized that it was incorporated into almost every building. The vaulted room, though dark and gloomy, also influenced much of the exterior architectural styling of Late Classic buildings.

Aside from considerations pertaining to construction problems encountered with vaulted rooms, it is necessary to consider their practical utility in serving the Maya on a day-to-day basis.

There is reason to believe that the rooms in the palaces and on top of the truncated pyramids provided only limited utility. The Maya then, as now, would have found it more advantageous and comfortable to live in easily constructed and well-ventilated huts having dirt floors and being made of poles and thatched roofs which could be located much closer to sources of domestic water than were usually available in the immediate vicinity of the elaborate ceremonial centers. Most of the stone structures were located on mounds somewhat remote from tillable land, and while it has been suggested that the Maya appreciated the view — which usually consisted of nothing but a green carpet of trees extending into infinity — considerations of view were undoubtedly the least-important thoughts of the average Maya of that time.

The vaulted rooms in the palaces would have been unlikely places for human abode due to inherent features. Not only were most of the stone structures placed on somewhat inaccessible mounds, but many of their rooms were found on the second, third and even higher floors of large structures. The preponderance of stone relegated most rooms to the category of damp holes; worse, very few of the vaulted rooms were equipped with vents whereby smoke from cooking and heating fires could manage to escape.

Many Maya palaces contained a structural feature which has received insufficient attention, mainly because excavation and restoration efforts have often failed to remove fallen debris down to the level of the building footings. We find that a very large number of room openings are located on a protruding stone ledge which usually varies from two to three feet above the normal ground level of many structures. To the short-of-stature Maya man or woman, the necessity of adding steps so that water, food and household items could be packed up and into a room would make little sense, nor would that barrier contribute to the ease of children running in and out of the house. The Maya did not then, nor do they now, see fit to abruptly separate the elevation of the inside of their homes from the adjoining exterior ground surfaces. To the Maya of Late Classic times, the openings in the vaulted rooms of the pyramids and palaces would have looked more like windows than doors.

If the Maya had intended their rooms to serve as living quarters or for storage purposes, it would have been a simple matter to have placed a flat roof across the room at the medial molding level or to have constructed a low-pitched roof for aesthetic or structural purposes. Either design would have been simple to construct and, of greater importance, the room would have served equally well for normal utilitarian purposes. To produce and veneer the boot-shaped facing stones against the steep, inward-sloping walls of the vault was no small task, and construction had to proceed slowly so as to permit the concrete to set behind the stones and in the core of the structure. Also, valuable smooth-faced building stones, which would have been desirable building materials in the construction of any ceremonial complex, were used in erecting the end walls of the vault and the inward-sloping portions of the ceiling. Where good-quality stones were not available, the ceiling and end walls of the vault, as well as the remainder of the room, were usually plastered. Often, the smooth-faced ceiling stones contained numerous carvings (as can be seen in the structures at "new" Chich'en Itzá) or, unexplainably, they were covered with a coat of painted plaster.

We have noted that architectural features of the various ceremonial centers were strongly influenced by the special characteristics of the bedded-stone deposits. Each of the five large ceremonial centers, as well as other lesser settlements, generally built with bedded stone or local caprock adorned with plaster, and architectural features were adapted to available building materials. Of peculiar significance, the vaulted room is found everywhere, and from a time preceding the Late Classic era on through and into Post Classic times (as at "new" Chich'en Itzá), we find a slavish adherence to its shape and interior finish. This feature of Maya construction, involving vaults which were either pointed at their apex or truncated by the placement of cross-stones just below the point of ceiling convergence, is found everywhere in Maya structures between 200 and 1200 A.D.

We must conclude that the suitability of most vaulted rooms for human habitation was simply nonexistent. Some of them might have been utilized to a limited extent for the storage of hides and skins, seeds, nuts, maize, beans, dried fruits, quetzal feathers, salt, smoked fish and meat, flint, obsidian, shells, and other goods for trade or long-term storage where protection from weather, birds, snakes and rodents was desired. Even so, the use of the rooms for storage purposes is suspect because there is little or no evidence in most instances that their rectangular-shaped openings had doors or other obstructions and, for that matter, entries supported by round columns, such as were constructed in the Grand Palace at Sayil and elsewhere, could not have been closed for such uses.

The height of the vaulted portion of most palace rooms usually bears a direct relationship to the ornamented exterior facade portion of the building located above the medial molding. It would be reasonable to believe that the elaborate facade of each building was its main attraction since it was exposed to view, and it would seem that the high, interior vaults, which were mostly dark and hidden from view, would have been built simply because there was space available. The disturbing feature of the foregoing analysis is that the additional difficulty of constructing the high, pointed or truncated vaults and their usual fine finish of shaped stone and/or plaster raises a suspicion that, perhaps, the vault was a very important feature of palaces and other structures. Accordingly, in view of the questions relating to why the vaults were built, we must ultimately turn to religious practices of the times in search of answers.

The pyramid obviously was sacred to the Maya; likewise, the vaulted room. On examination, we find the interior vault to be nearly identical with the slope and shape of the pyramid, and it is logical to believe that the pyramid and the vault complemented each other in the religious expression of the times. We may never know for certain, but the vaulted rooms may have been as important as abodes for their gods as the pyramids. When we examine the Funerary Crypt of Pacal at Palenque, it can be noted that, rather than utilizing a compact cubicle for his remains, a vaulted room was constructed within and at the bottom of the Pyramid of the Inscriptions. Vaulted rooms almost always were an essential part of Late Classic pyramids and palaces.

Most of the vaulted rooms were undoubtedly devoted to their gods and related religious activities, serving as places for instruction and training, initiation ceremonies, performances of secret rites, storage of religious costumes, and the display of pictures, paintings and

151

artifacts. Double rooms, where the rear portions contained openings at a higher elevation, probably contained figures which were objects of worship.

(b) A Millenium of Temple Building Ends

Up to this point I have avoided classifying some Maya pyramids and buildings as temples; at other times, I have occasionally made qualifying references, such as "pyramid temples." The reason may be that history has impressed upon us a mental image which dictates that a temple should incorporate the high and many-columned architectural features of those found in Egypt and Greece. And the fact that the Maya built structures which, in the eyes of those of us who have inherited European standards, give an appearance of palaces, can easily provide misleading impressions.

The Late Classic Maya often were unable to find slabs of stone of sufficient length to span the openings of their vaulted rooms, thus limiting the width of the openings or necessitating the laborious job of hewing hardwood beams to serve as lintels. Accordingly, the only non-stone ingredient in many structures in the five major ceremonial centers was a single, hardwood lintel placed across each room opening. And in those cases where a slab of stone could be secured, the support strength of the slab was limited because the grain of the stone, as laid down horizontally during its formation, did not provide as much strength as would have been the case if the stone could have been broken or cut to a proper size and then laid on edge. Accordingly, much of the structural failure encountered over the period of several hundred years was due to the collapse of decaying wood or broken stone lintels in the many buildings.

We can see the final expression of Maya architecture when it terminated under the Toltec influence at Chich'en Itzá about 1200 A.D.. In a single structure a short distance from the Observatory, there can be seen the remains of what to the mind of the average reader is a building which more nearly resembles the kind of temple we have been looking for. A rectangular structure with several openings in the wall along its one exposed long side, it contains three long, parallel rooms. The three rooms are not separated by walls as typical Maya construction

This three-vaulted temple built by the Toltec-Maya in the "old" section of Chich'en Itzá utilized round columns instead of solid concrete-and-stone walls to support the vaulted roof structure. Note the double hardwood beams (cut off during restoration) which spanned across the columns to support the roof structure.

dictated; rather, the entire interior consists of round stone columns, each capped with a flat, square stone. The span across the top of the columns was too long to be bridged with available stone slabs, so a double row of heavy hardwood beams, each beam being nearly a foot square and about eight or nine feet long, was placed across the top of the capstones of the columns. Thus, at room height, there were two exterior long walls and two parallel interior rows of columns, the capstone of each interior row being bridged by the double hardwood beams. The roof was then placed upon the four parallel supporting walls and columns so constructed.

The partially restored structure furnishes evidence that the major architectural change encountered in shifting from a solid wall to a

The partially restored Temple of the Warriors as visitors view it today. The entire vaulted roof structure is missing.

column-type support system on the interior of the building did not coincide with any compensating architectural change in the roof construction. Instead of a flat roof being placed across the structure at room height as we might now expect would have been adopted, the Maya adhered to the long-used vaulted interior ceiling. By using all four of the vertical support walls and columns, three long, parallel ceiling vaults were constructed, with two of the stone-and-concrete portions of the roof system being placed upon the hardwood beams extending along the top of the two interior columns.

Late Classic construction in the Puuc area provides us with temple-like structures at two conspicuous places: the Venus Temple located at the lower left corner of the north building of the Quadrangle at Uxmal, and the second level of the Grand Palace at Sayil. However, under the Toltec influence at Chich́en Itźa, there are many structures

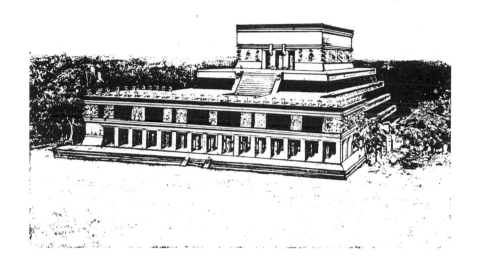

The Temple of the Warriors as it probably looked when built (ca 1100-1200 A.D.)

which utilized square or round columns, providing a temple-like appearance and furnishing open access to their interiors. The crowning achievement of the Toltec-Maya temple construction is, of course, the Temple of the Warriors. In fact, Morris estimated that there were more than 65 hewn beams averaging nine feet in length in the superstructure of the Temple of the Warriors alone.

The Toltec-Maya opted for a fragile-type support system for the overlaying vaults and roof mass by eliminating supporting walls and utilizing round or square stone columns. Whereas most Maya room openings were limited to a maximum of about five or six feet, the column spans at Chich'en Itzá during Toltec-Maya times were often eight to twelve feet, and so the builders modified their construction techniques by placing double rows of hardwood beams above the columns.

From an engineering standpoint, placing the load of the vaulted ceiling area and the remainder of the roof mass upon the hardwood beams should have provided clear warning that the collapse of the hardwood beams (which was most likely to eventually occur due to rotting or sagging) would bring down the entire roof; from a construction standpoint, a very delicate balancing act was involved in placing the common concrete leg of two parallel vaults upon the hardwood beams.

That the Maya chose to incorporate a structural flaw into their temples in order to retain the seemingly useless vaulted ceiling areas is further proof of the religious importance of the vault.

It may have been that the structural defect of utilizing hardwood beams as column spanners did not concern the builders, but when Morris arrived at Chich'en Itz'a in 1925 to restore the Temple of the Warriors, he observed that there was not a single colonnade built by the Toltec-Maya which had retained its roof structure. The hardwood beams had rotted and collapsed, with the great roof mass falling among the columns, many of which were left standing in their original positions.

No more would Maya construction be dominated by the vaulted room. Its era had come to a close. Later Post Classic construction at Tulum adopted the flat ceiling, occasioned at least in substantial measure by the absence at the site of bedded-stone deposits from which superior stone could be secured.

Many students and tourists visit Chich'en Itz'a today, and they marvel at the skeleton of the Temple of the Warriors. But they would marvel even more if they could see that temple as it must have really looked when it was completed. The Toltec influence on the Maya may have had undesirable features, but an honest appraisal of their stone-working techniques, considered in the light of the nature of the available stone deposit, requires an assessment that much of their influence was not negative.

(d) *Ruins in Strange Places*

The logical explanation for the existence of the great ceremonial centers under discussion is that they were built for religious and closely related purposes, with trading, storage and administrative uses being secondary. Why, then, were they located in such unlikely and inhospitable places? By now, the answer should be clear: The five major ceremonial centers (including the satellite Puuc sites beyond Uxmal) were located where the Maya found large deposits of bedded stone. With remarkable tenacity, they sought out the special resource which enabled them to display their talents and to construct mighty monuments pleasing to their gods.

Once it is understood that the Maya built ceremonial centers where they could find deposits of bedded stone, we should not fall back into the trap of believing the size of a ceremonial center was an indicator of population numbers in the surrounding countryside. Again, the extent of the available stone deposits determined the physical size of each ceremonial center. The number of people living around any particular ceremonial center could have been, and often very likely was, entirely disproportionate to the physical size of the complex.

It is tempting to wander afield in search of parallel situations where important ruins have been found in remote and relatively inaccessible locations. For purposes of comparison, we will examine the Egyptian monument of Abu Simbel and the Inca fortress city of Machu Picchu in Peru.

Like the Yucatan Peninsula, most of Egypt was once submerged in a shallow sea, and at different locations there were laid down thick, bedded deposits of both limestone and sandstone. Many of the great temples built by the Egyptians between approximately 1200 and 2500 B.C. along the Nile River in central Egypt utilized bedded sandstone deposits, and in many of their structures we find blocks of sandstone which, on being measured, show one layer to have been approximately 18 to 20 inches thick and another thicker layer of approximately 42 inches. As might be expected, most of the great temples of Egypt can be found along the fertile Nile River where settled populations have existed for thousands of years.

An anomolous situation exists at Abu Simbel, near the southern border of Egypt and a short distance below the second cataract of the Nile. In an area where the river valley was narrow and where a limited

Located 180 miles up river from Aswan, Egypt, the Temple of Abu Simbel was carved from a monolithic sandstone deposit. The temple is found behind the 67-foot high seated figures. The entire structure was dismantled and moved to higher ground to escape the rising waters impounded behind the High Aswan dam.

group of herders supported themselves from livestock grazing activities, the question has been raised (but apparently not answered) as to why Pharaoh Ramesses II came to that desolate spot shortly after 1300 B.C. and directed a host of workmen to create the four huge, seated figures of himself guarding the entrance to a large underground temple with numerous rooms containing paintings depicting his alleged military triumphs over the Hittites. When one understands the desire of the Egyptian pharaohs to glorify themselves (while ostensibly honoring their gods) and to prepare for the next life, it seems rather easy to explain the existence of the massive undertaking at Abu Simbel. The attraction at Abu Simbel, unlike the situation farther down the Nile River, was that the craftsmen of Egypt found a large and unusual monolithic sandstone deposit near the river *which was not bedded*. When one works in a quarry with bedded stone, the idea is to effect a separation of stone slabs along the horizontal bedding planes; but at Abu Simbel the craftsmen knew they could carve huge figures, including rooms within the hillside, without the risk of the entire structure slipping and falling apart along seam lines which would have been found in other sandstone deposits. That particular deposit was worked with bronze tools rather easily and, like the Maya — but for a somewhat different purpose — the Egyptians built the monolithic stone edifice at another site sparsely populated and only occasionally visited. They could not move the solid sandstone deposit to a different location, so they constructed on-site and subsequently abandoned their work to the ages.

. . . .

A slow, three-hour train ride in a northwesterly direction from Cusco, Peru, the center of the Inca empire and the oldest existing city in the Western Hemisphere, takes one down the Urubumba River to the abandoned city of Machu Picchu. During the last 30 miles of the route, the train hugs the mountain along the gorge of the river as it roars out of the Andes Mountains on its journey to join the Amazon River.

The last mile of the trip prior to reaching the ruins reveals a complete change of geologic formations. Huge, thick layers of white granite (andesite) cling almost vertically to mountain pinnacles on both sides of the canyon walls, indicating violent volcanic action at some time in the distant past. At the railroad terminus, it is necessary to utilize small buses to traverse a switchback road which takes visitors to the ruins located on a high ridge far above the river. At an altitude of 8,200 feet, the ruins are dwarfed by yet higher peaks extending like pointed fingers reaching into the sky.

Machu Picchu is located in one of the most rugged and desolate spots on earth, and the trails which bound it to other Inca outposts would have been unbelievably treacherous and devoid of human settlements for great distances. The small fortress city was built sometime about 1400 A.D., and it was occupied by about 500 inhabitants for approximately 200 years until abandoned shortly after the Spanish Con-

The small abandoned city of Machu Picchu is found in the lower reaches of the Peruvian Andes at an elevation of 8,200 feet. Note the large, flat slabs of andesite granite hanging vertically to the peak immediately behind and to the right of the ruins.

quest.

Most of the stone found in the Andes Mountains and valleys is of volcanic origin, and for that reason the inhabitants have had only limited access to sedimentary-type building stone deposits, such as limestones, sandstones and quartzites, which are often bedded and can be pried loose in the form of slabs. At Machu Picchu the Inca found volcanic-formed slabs and chunks of white granite on a high ridge where the forces of nature had broken them into many large and small pieces, a substantial number of which had at least one reasonably smooth side. Since the broken stones lay loose in a massive heap along the top of the ridge, rather than being a solid unstratified deposit which would have been impossible to quarry with the tools and teachnology of the times, it was possible for the Inca to address each separate stone, whatever its size, and work the stone into smaller stones having desired sizes and shapes.

By 1350 A.D. the Inca had access to bronze metal tools, so they were able to work the granite by splitting large stones into smaller blocks by the process of driving a series of metal wedges along a straight line and then pounding the wedges in unison so as to produce a clean, straight break when the stone popped open. By way of background, the high country of Peru and Bolivia had ample deposits of tin and copper, each metal being relatively soft; however, when tin (10%-15%) was alloyed with copper (90%-85%), bronze was created. Bronze was much harder than either of its metal components, and it produced suitable tools for splitting and abrading the white granite found in Inca country.

The granite at both Cusco and Machu Picchu had a somewhat unusual composition in that it was uniformly interspersed with small, hard nodules at approximately quarter-inch intervals, with the interstitial spaces consisting of soft areas of equal size, thus making for a consistent texture which was half-hard, half-soft. As a result, the stone could be split along fairly straight lines with the use of wedges and, as an added advantage, the nature of its composition allowed it to be pounded or abraded rather easily with metal hammers, notwithstanding its somewhat illusory appearance of extreme hardness. This allowed the Inca to produce the flat, straight bedding surfaces for which the stone work at Machu Picchu and in and around Cusco has become famous.

Where loose deposits of broken granite could be found in locations such as Machu Picchu and on the mountain above Cusco, the Inca of the 14th and 15th centuries made building blocks which were used to form solid bearing walls for a limited number of buildings. Bearing walls require stone blocks with a substantial bonding surface on the bottom and top of each block and, lacking limestone from which they could make cement mortar and concrete, the success of Inca wall construction depended upon fitting the stones together with little or no tolerance. Some of the walls were constructed without any bonding material between the mating stones; on other walls it can be observed that a very thin layer of mud clay was utilized as a bonding agent.

The Inca at Machu Picchu built stone dwellings on the steep ridge far above the muddy Urubumba River.

By far the greater amount of stone-work at Machu Picchu and throughout the high country occupied by the Inca involved the construction of retaining walls built on steep slopes so as to provide small plots of land which could be farmed. The stone used for that purpose was rubble rock, of which there was an ample supply, and the durability of the retaining walls depended upon the skill of the stone fitters who had no mortar or concrete.

The majority of Inca stone structures are devoid of architectural interest, and they lack the elaborate ornamentation and other beautiful features of Late Classic Maya stone-work. We need not be concerned with whether the Inca could have equalled the skill and artistry of their Maya cousins since they were working with completely different stones and building materials from those available to the

Maya, and they were subject to the limitations of the materials available to them.

The extremely steep mountain slopes at Machu Picchu severely limited food supplies secured from hunting and gathering. Nor were there any fertile valleys nearby from which agricultural crops could be produced. The Inca were almost totally dependent upon narrow, terraced plots of land surrounding their small city. It is amazing that the few acres gleaned from steep, terraced slopes of 45° to 60° could have produced even minimal food supplies for the small population. Despite the obstacles of terrain and distance, Machu Picchu probably secured maize and other staple food products from other distant Inca settlements from time to time. It is not surprising that when the Spaniards cut off contact with other Inca communities after they reached Cusco in 1530 A.D., it became an isolated outpost. Its fate was sealed, and in a relatively short period of time it, too, became another ghost town of the ages.

Machu Picchu was constructed where it was primarily because of the unusual and large deposit of loose stone which was found on the ridge above the present ruins. Its construction during the Inca reign coincided with the development of a technology which provided metal tools with which to work the available stone. Although it was in fact a small city, the restrictions of an inadequate food supply constantly threatened its existence and set the stage for its eventual abandonment when that delicate balance was upset. Machu Picchu has provided us with another example of great stone works being constructed where workable stone was available, only to be abandoned when the laws of survival took precedence.

Whenever and wherever on earth man has found a workable deposit of building stone, he has always managed to create some struc ture with it, whether it had a practical use or not.

The Toltec-Maya built the Temple of the Jaguar at "new" Chichén Itzá (ca. 1100-1200 A.D.).

POST-CLASSIC CHICHÉN ITZÁ

We have been told that construction at all of the ceremonial centers terminated by 900 A.D. or shortly thereafter, except at Chichén Itzá where two distinct periods of construction had taken place. The "old" portion, which lies mostly south of the road which formerly intersected the ruins, was constructed during Late Classic times; the "new" portion, which is found mostly on the north side of the former road, dates to a period approximating 1100-1200 A.D. Unlike the "old" portion, which contained several buildings with mosaic patterns, the "new" portion was influenced by the Toltecs who came into the area at the later date. The last construction phase utilized thicker layers of bedded stone, with the usual percentage of waste rubble available for pyramid use. The lack of reasonable quantities of thin layers of bedded stone seems to have discouraged the use of mosaic patterns on structures found in the "new" portion.

Recent research has placed the Toltecs in the northern reaches of the Valley of Mexico (approximately 50 miles north of Mexico City) at the site of Tula (Tollan). Reputedly, the Toltecs occupied the site with another group with which they were in conflict much of the time. As a result, sometime around 950 A.D. the tribe departed the area under the leadership of Kukulcan, the "Plumed Serpent," and migrated into the Gulf Coast area. They eventually found their way into the northern Yucatan Peninsula, where they established themselves. The Toltecs brought different religious practices and new gods to add to those of the Maya, and eventually Kukulcan acquired the status of a god.

Maya tradition insists that Kukulcan (called Quetzalcóatl by the Aztecs) brought the arts and sciences of civilization to the Western Hemisphere, and that he built Chich'en Itz'a. In sorting out the murky facets of the legend, it seems that Kukulcan built "new" Chich'en Itz'a with the assistance of a "bearded white personage" who had come by boat from across the sea from which the sun rises. After Chich'en Itz'a had been built, according to some versions of the legend, the "bearded white personage" returned by boat to his homeland across the sea. The Maya and the Aztecs both awaited the return of their god in human form in the year 1519, ironically, the same year that Cortez and his conquering army reached Tenochtitlán (the present site of Mexico City). The Aztecs offered no resistance, mistakenly believing that Cortez was the god they were expecting.

(a) *New Stone-Working Tools*

Post Classic construction at "new" Chich'en Itz'a (1100-1200 A.D.) represents a significant departure from much of the stone-work of Late Classic times in the following respects:

(1) Numerous large, cube-shaped blocks of stone containing precision-formed, right-angled corners;

(2) The use of a substantial number of round columns;

(3) A large number of hewn hardwood beams used to span room openings;

(4) A profusion of deep, intricate carvings of elaborate designs, both upon wall facing stones and in creating large serpent heads and other objects; and

(5) The appearance of a substantial number of wall facing stones of considerably greater dimensions than found elsewhere.

The Toltec-Maya continued to use facing blocks which were created by the previously outlined breaking process applied to layered slabs which predominated the construction method of the Late Classic era. But the "new" portion of Chich'en Itzá introduced different architectural designs which were foreign in many respects to Late Classic construction, except for a few parallel examples which can be found in the Puuc Hills area at the very end of Late Classic construction.

The limestone found in the bedded deposits at "new" Chich'en Itzá differed from the Puuc limestone in that it was both harder and found in thicker layers. Whereas Puuc construction utilized several layers of limestone between four inches and ten inches in thickness which could be used for mosaic patterns, it appears that several of the layers at "new" Chich'en Itzá were considerably thicker. The thickness of the various layers can be determined by taking vertical measurements of the blocks in the square columns of the Temple of the Warriors.

The bedded-stone layers at the Puuc sites were more "chalky" in appearance, softer, and easier to work. The Puuc limestone was also characterized by the presence of small amounts of iron oxides which produced shades of cream, gold, orange and pink. In addition, much of the Puuc limestone contained small, discrete objects interspersed throughout the stone, suggesting a somewhat different geologic formation. On the other hand, the layers of limestone at "new" Chich'en Itzá retained their soft buff coloration, which turned grey upon exposure to the weather. That limestone, as well as being thicker, was con-

Square columns in the Temple of the Warriors.

siderably harder than the Puuc limestone, even to the point of being slightly marbleized.

When we compare the quality of workmanship and the quantity and dimension of construction at Chich'en Itz'a, it is readily apparent that the Toltec-Maya who built "new" Chich'en Itz'a appeared to have been more proficient in specific techniques than the Late Classic Maya who built "old" Chich'en Itz'a. Further, the size of their structures and the use of larger individual stones suggests an even more-pronounced ability on the part of the Toltec-Maya. Accordingly, we must ask ourselves whether the Toltecs brought better stone-working techniques and tools to Maya country when they established headquarters at "new" Chich'en Itz'a.

One can examine the structures built by the inhabitants of the highland valleys of Mexico, extending from Oaxaca on the south northerly to the upper reaches of the Valley of Mexico (i.e., Tula and Teotihuacán), and it will be noted that, except for a few large pyramids, almost all of the structures were low-profile and the use of enclosed rooms was very limited. In fact, except for a few narrow passageways found in some of the structures at Monte Albán, the highland peoples made no attempt to construct vaulted rooms. The general method of wall construction consisted of rubble stone held together with a concrete mixture, and usually plastered.

The highland peoples depended primarily upon volcanic-type stones for construction purposes, some of which were very hard and unusable while others were soft and workable. Limestone deposits were present at scattered locations, but they were used to produce cement for bonding the low walls together. The sculpture work at Teotihuacán, Tenochtitlán (at a later date), and at Tula utilized large chunks of volcanic stone which could be pounded and abraded so as to produce serpent heads, statues, and similar objects. Much of the volcanic stone so used, being somewhat soft in texture, has deteriorated badly over the many years.

With specific reference to Tula, the Toltecs built an original version of the Temple of the Warriors at Tula before they abandoned the site. They utilized both round and square columns, but the columns — as well as the facing walls of their temple — were constructed of rubble rock, held together with a concrete mixture and plastered for aesthetic effect. Nothing in the construction at Tula furnishes us with any indication that the Toltecs were nearly as capable as the Maya when it came to architectural or stone-working abilities.

A critical comparison of the stone ruins of the highland country, including Monte Albán at Oaxaca, Tenochtitlán (later built at the site of present-day Mexico City by the Aztecs), Teotihuacán (located approximately 30 miles north of Mexico City), and Tula (another 20 miles farther north and beyond Teotihuacán), mandates the inescapable conclusion that the Maya of the Yucatan were more advanced architecturally and possessed stone-working techniques which were far superior to those of their mountain cousins. Undoubtedly, the special bedded-stone deposits of the Yucatan Peninsula were a contributing factor to Maya superiority.

Since it is extremely unlikely that the Toltecs were able to enlarge upon the skills and abilities of the local Maya of the northern Yucatan Peninsula, it is difficult to explain why the second-phase construction techniques at Chich'en Itzá were so much more advanced beyond those of the Late Classic Maya. The problem is compounded because I am convinced that the Toltec-Maya took over and mastered the bedded-stone deposits which the Late Classic Maya were forced to abandon before they were completely utilized.

Considering the texture, hardness, density and the thickness of the excellent-quality limestone layers available to the builders of "new" Chich'en Itzá, I reluctantly accept the distinct probability that the cube-shaped blocks in the columns of the Temple of the Warriors (and other structures) and the many round columns surrounding and in the vicinity of the Temple of the Warriors (and elsewhere) could not have been made with stone tools alone or by any other natural means available to their builders. For reasons which will be developed as we move along, the persistent stories that Kukulcan built "new" Chich'en Itzá with the assistance of the "bearded white personage" must be considered in a new light. If the Toltec-Maya did have access to metal tools, it is my opinion that they had to have been made of steel and of sizes and shapes which any Western Hemisphere metallurgy of the times could not have produced.

At all times during the Late Classic era at all of the five major ceremonial centers, stone construction primarily involved the quarrying of stone slabs and reducing them to individual stones with square or rectangular faces by a breaking, shaping and trimming process. Cube-shaped blocks and specially shaped or carved stones were not produced in large quantities, and such as were needed were usually produced by careful sorting and what we might term "lucky" breaks. The process was further simplified in locations such as the Puuc Hills, where much of the layered stone was less thick, and at Cop'an, where the tuffaceous nature of the stone and its bedding characteristics both contributed to its easy workability.

Archaeological research at Chich'en Itzá indicates that the "new" portion was built in part in the same area as the "old" portion and that the time differential between the two construction phases might

The Toltec-Maya built the Observatory in the "old" portion of Chich'en Itz'a on top of a structure previously built by the Late Classic Maya.

have been as much as 200 years or more. That situation was not completely without precedent during Late Classic times, but we are constrained to wonder why the Late Classic Maya did not quarry and use the excellent stone at Chich'en Itz'a and, instead, waited for the Toltec arrival to assist them in completing the job. Aside from the lack of substantial quantities of thin layers which could be used for mosaic pieces, the somewhat thicker layers of bedded stone in the central and northern portion of the deposit contained stone of good quality and uniform consistency. As such, that stone was very desirable and suitable for use.

It is my opinion that the Maya initially bypassed those portions of that stone deposit because they lacked the manpower and necessary tools to adequately quarry, size and trim that stone into desired shapes. As they proceeded to the north with their quarrying activities, they undoubtedly encountered a stratum of overburden caprock which became increasingly thick, actually exceeding four feet in thickness. That particular layer had to be removed in order to quarry and use the less-thick and better underlying layers which were desirable for construction purposes, and that obstacle would have been a major consideration in convincing the Maya of Late Classic times to avoid the remainder of the deposit. Notwithstanding more than 500 years of sophisticated stone-working techniques developed during Late Classic times, the arrival of the Toltecs somehow introduced superior techniques of quarrying and shaping stone.

It is quite possible that the Toltecs secured and brought with them a limited number of basic steel tools.

Fire-hardened sticks and poles were inadequate to accomplish the job of separating the thick stratum of overburden which rested upon desirable bedded layers beneath, and it was only possible to pry huge chunks loose along vertical cracks created by the forces of nature by using steel tools. I am not referring to small bronze or iron objects which might possibly have been created by smelting processes somewhere in the Western Hemisphere; rather, the task required the availability of a few steel crowbars with pointed or chisel-shaped ends, being five or six feet in length and having solid shanks of at least one and one-half inches diameter. The better caprock stone of proper sizes was then available to be made into huge serpent heads and similar objects; the less-desirable stone, or rubble, could find its way into a pyramid or be buried somewhere in a plaza area.

After bedded-stone layers were exposed and made available, the Toltec-Maya undertook the ambitious and delicate task of creating an unusually large number of cube-shaped blocks for the columns of the Temple of the Warriors and for the corner columns of their walls, room openings, and various other applications. As previously noted, the thickness of the available quarried slabs also dictated the vertical thickness of the numerous cube-shaped blocks which went into the columns of the Temple of the Warriors, many of which weigh a thousand pounds or more. An inspection of the blocks reveals that the four companion corners of each block which had to be formed by human effort are usually straight and invariably at right angles to each other. Also, the horizontal measurements of each block correspond closely with those of the other blocks constituting each column.

Similar precise construction standards apply to the numerous exposed corner stones of the walls, room openings, stairways and other features at "new" Chich'en Itz'a. In fact, all of the cube-shaped stones exhibit superior craftsmanship and are generally longer than those found at "old" Chich'en Itz'a and the other major ceremonial centers of the Yucatan Peninsula.

To determine how the Toltec-Maya were able to produce cube-shaped stones in the quantity and of the quality found at "new" Chich'en Itz'a with only stone tools presents questions for which there are no simple answers. The hardness of the limestone at "new" Chich'en Itz'a, even when freshly exposed to the elements, coupled with other factors which I have previously enumerated, long ago convinced me that each separate block could not have been produced by chipping and pecking methods.

One possible method of producing cube-shaped blocks might have involved drilling or scribing narrow grooves along a stone so that sharp, pointed stone wedges could have been inserted and pounded until a section of stone broke loose. That method, however, would have been highly unlikely to produce the straight breaks encountered; at least, the chances of achieving straight breaks would have been minimal. I have searched extensively among all of the five major ceremonial centers for evidence which would indicate that the Maya separated any of their stone by the wedge method, but I have never been able to find a single indication of the existence of wedge grooves or other marks.

The difficulty with the standard method of creating smooth facing stones by the use of a green hardwood pole or any other natural device, as previously indicated, was the inability to control the direction of the break beyond the surface of the stone; in short, that method had severe limitations when it came to producing right-angled corners so necessary to producing cube-shaped blocks.

I can only conclude that the four man-made sides of the cube-shaped blocks we have been discussing could have been made by one of three methods, all of which would have entailed the use of tools or objects made of steel:

FIRST, the blocks could have been manually sawed with a coarse cable or similar flexible strand of metal, possibly with the application of water; or

SECOND, two workers on each end of a cross-cut saw, together with the possible application of water, could have slowly and carefully sawed the four sides of each block; or

THIRD, a steel rod, identical to the crowbar previously mentioned except for having a three-inch or four-inch square plate on the pounding end, could have produced a reasonable number of cube-shaped blocks if the slab from which the block was being made was placed on (and beyond) another slab having a solid, straight edge and, further, another straight-edge slab of stone was placed on top of the subject slab so that heavy, concentrated blows could be carefully directed along a narrow shear line so as to finally produce a clean, straight break.

I view the first possibility as being somewhat unlikely to have occurred, but either of the second or third methods would have been possible.

When Earl Morris was restoring the Temple of the Warriors, he produced cube-shaped blocks by cutting the non-abrasive limestone with a simple cross-cut saw which he attached to the rear wheel of a Model T Ford which had been jacked up and connected to the saw so as to produce a steady forward-and-backward motion. Similarly, two men on each end of a saw also could have accomplished that job.

As for the third method, modern hydraulic stone-cutting devices are able to break lengths of stone by inserting slabs between two sharp edges and then applying a sudden burst of pressure from above, thus causing the stone to shear along a straight line. A manual process whereby the force of short, solid blows could be similarly focused and

It is believed that the many stone columns near the Temple of the Warriors supported a perishable roof structure which housed a market.

directed, although much less effective, would have been reasonably practical and effective.

In the construction of the Temple of the Warriors and its connected facilities, the Toltec-Maya created approximately 1,000 round stone columns, most of which were the same height as the square columns. The cube-shaped blocks for the square columns were undoubtedly the premier product of all stone-shaping activities at "new" Chich'en Itzá, and it is apparent that a bad break on any one of the right-angled companion corners of a particular block would relegate that stone to being used for a round column. The measurements which I took of the diameter of the various columns all indicate that the circumference of the various stones in the columns would fit within the overall dimensions of similar stones which were used for square columns. Accordingly, a bad break on a cube-shaped stone would usually leave that stone available for use as a round column stone.

Although Late Classic Maya construction furnishes evidence of some round stone columns, particularly in the Puuc area, the Toltec-Maya were dealing with a considerably harder limestone and, in addition, the volume of round columns found around and in the vicinity of the Temple of the Warriors is so great that I must also discard any consideration that either pecking or pounding was the method employed. Again, after due consideration, I must conclude that the many round columns were created in their final form by utilizing steel rasps or coarse files, objects which, as we shall note, could have been available.

As previously noted, temple construction by the Toltec-Maya took on a much more-open appearance by the utilization of pairs of side-by-side hardwood beams, many of which were 10 to 12 feet in length and averaging about 12 inches square. The various structures built by the Toltec-Maya at "new" Chich'en Itz'a, including the Temple of the Warriors, probably required as many as 150 hewn beams.

Restoration efforts have replaced many of the beams which rotted and collapsed over the centuries, including the replacement of short sections of beams into the wall cavities where the originals were placed so as to furnish visitors with a reasonably accurate representation of how the structures were constructed. Occasionally, however, the original beams have been cut off, leaving short sections anchored in the concrete matrix of the bearing wall. A careful inspection of the paired remnant sections suggests that the undersides of some of the beams which were placed upon stone or concrete surfaces, as well as the parallel mating sides, may have sometimes been sawed, but exposure to the elements over the many years makes it virtually impossible to determine whether or not all of the beams were hewn or whether portions of some of them may have been created with a metal saw.

To secure and shape hardwood beams would have normally entailed a far greater expenditure of effort than would have been employed in producing an equal volume of stone lintels. After selecting a suitable tree, the task of cutting it down, removing limbs and bark, and trimming and shaping it into a long retangular beam which would match up against a companion beam would have been a major task. The availability of a crosscut saw or, more likely, a grubbing-type or ordinary flat axe would have greatly simplified the task and reduced the necessary labor output to a small fraction of what would have been required with the use of stone tools. The availability of metal tools for producing hardwood beams would have greatly encouraged their use, and the presence of so many beams suggests that metal saws and axes were available to the Toltec-Maya.

Construction at "new" Chich'en Itz'a is further distinguished from that of the Late Classic era by a voluminous amount of detailed, elaborate carvings of various types. The use of stelae and mosaics was abandoned in favor of a different architectural style which featured greater pictorial expression. The interior walls, and even the vaulted ceilings, of many enclosed structures feature incised carvings depicting their lifestyle and religious beliefs and practices. The Toltec-Maya were not content to furnish the interior of their vaulted rooms with smooth facing stones; rather, they often went to the extra work of carving the same stones, as can be found in the Temple of the Jaguar, the square columns in the Temple of the Warriors, and in the North Temple at the end of the Ball Court. The walls of several exterior structures were equally ornamented with similar carvings, as can be seen on the sidewalls of the Temple of the Warriors, the Temple of the Tables, portions of the Ball Court, the South Temple of the Ball Court, and the Tzompantli (wall of skulls).

Further, the Toltec-Maya carved chacmools, jaguars and numerous serpent heads from large, individual blocks of limestone, displaying the ability to work and shape large blocks of stone into objects containing numerous difficult-to-reach areas.

To perform the voluminous amount of elaborate carvings, each carefully and deeply etched into relatively hard limestone, preponderates in favor of an assessment that pointed steel objects or chisels were used for cutting and etching purposes, assisted by metal hammers.

Lastly, although the Toltec-Maya continued to produce wall facing stones where the bonding surfaces were not at right angles to the

The Chacmool at Chichén Itzá was associated with an imported sacrificial rite where the warm, beating heart of the victim was torn from his chest and then carried by a racing messenger to the reclining form of the idol, there to be placed in a receptacle clasped in its hands. The Toltecs and other tribes located in the Valley of Mexico featured the Chacmool in their religious rites.

OPPOSITE: Serpent heads guard the stairway of the Platform of the Tigers and Eagles.

exposed faces, we find a definite tendency to larger stones as evidenced on portions of the Ball Court walls and both the interior and exterior portions of the Temple of the Jaguar. Facing stones at the other major ceremonial centers typically have exposed surfaces of 250 square inches or less (i.e., approximately 15 inches square, or the equivalent).

Numerous wall facing blocks at "new" Chich'en Itzá reveal measurements as much as two feet square, with many facing blocks having surface areas ranging between 300 to 500 square inches each. The nature of the available limestone being worked was certainly a contributing factor to the larger sizes of the facing stones; likewise, the availability of better tools cannot be ignored.

(b) *The Legend of the Bearded Man*

We must inquire of the source of metal tools available to the Maya at a time which must have been 300 to 600 years before the arrival of Columbus (i.e., 900-1200 A.D.). At some point during the 1300s, it

appears that the Inca alloyed tin and copper to create bronze tools, but it is doubtful that they were imported into Maya country or that the tools of that date would have been sufficiently developed for the job at hand. Further, it seems certain that any tools which the Inca may have manufactured would have postdated Chich'en Itzá. Logically, if metal tools capable of working stone had been produced in the Western Hemisphere during the time frame we have been discussing, there surely would be some evidence of their use for common pursuits in the form of shovels, hoes, knives, axes, spears, etc. Such evidence is lacking.

The Yucatan Peninsula has always been without deposits of iron, tin and copper, so we must exclude any consideration that some local cottage industry might have produced metal stone-working tools. And even as late as the Spanish Conquest, the Aztecs apparently had not developed metallurgy beyond the point of extracting, shaping and alloying copper, silver and gold into ornamental objects. I can only conclude that the Toltec-Maya secured metal stone-working tools from boats which crossed the Atlantic, most likely from a Mediterranean or a northern European source.

It is necessary at this point to again enlarge the area of our background observations in order to properly focus upon critical events leading up to the arrival of the Spaniards in the New World. Until the time of Columbus, seafaring nations sailed the oceans to a degree which, as information is constantly being advanced by new discoveries, tends to amaze us today. For several thousand years boats sailed far beyond established population centers; not for pleasure, not for two-way commerce, not usually for colonization — but to secure precious metals and ores. Although there can be no question that limited colonization efforts took place from time to time at earlier dates, it was not until the time of Columbus (1492) that economic pressures became so great that the nations of Europe embarked on a program of empire building as a means of disbursing expanding populations. It was in 1492 that the Spanish Inquisition expelled the Jews; it was in 1492 that the Spaniards evicted the Moors from the fabulous Alhambra at Granada and forced them to return to Africa; and it was the "discovery" in 1492 which enabled the tough, hungry Conquistadoras from the hills and plains of the Extremadura and Castilla-Leon regions of western Spain to acquire guns and horses and depart for the New World, there to plunder, steal and kill in search of fortunes.

When Columbus arrived at the temporary royal headquarters established at Santa Fe (near Granada) in 1492 to sell Ferdinand and Isabella on the idea of grubstaking his journey to America, he knew full-well that other boats had preceded him across the Atlantic to a new continent. The proof is evident in translated writings which can be observed in the Archives of the Indies building at Seville, Spain. And we can be certain that he presented a glowing promise of gold and other precious metals which could be obtained with slight effort. Ferdinand and Isabella were in the process of evicting the Moors from Granada, and they had numerous problems of state which occupied their time, with the result that the appeal made by Columbus was summarily rejected. However, the royal couple had an astute adviser — Louis de Santangel, "keeper of the privy purse" — who, on second thought, convinced his rulers that the wild promises made by Columbus might have merit and that Spain ought to grubstake a few craft, particularly so if secondary assistance might be secured from some speculative-minded merchants in providing the necessary vessels and supplies. Such an arrangement would cost the monarchy nothing and, in an event, what was there to be lost?

A messenger intercepted the departing Columbus at the nearby town of Pinos Puente, located a few miles from Granada, before noon of the next day, giving him the news that he had a deal. The agreement made on that day must be recognized as possibly the most eventful decision in recorded history. It led to the "discovery" of America, with the Spanish Crown becoming an active partner to the extent of approximately 20% of all gold and other precious metals arriving through the port of Seville from the New World. But the greatest impact occurred in the resulting colonization of the New World by Spain and other leading European nations — an exodus which has spanned nearly 500 years.

If Columbus had been motivated primarily by a belief that the earth was round and that one could reach the East Indies or Japan simply by sailing into the sunset, we would expect that he would have sailed due west from Cadiz, eventually reaching North America in the vicinity of Cape Hatteras. This route would have seemed plausible since Portuguese navigators had sailed to the Azores as early as 1427 — one-third of the distance to America. But Columbus had the benefit of a substantial amount of maritime experience — including maps — which had been accumulated and handed down over a period of many years and, instead, he opted for a route which took his three craft southwesterly along the west coast of Africa to the Canary Islands, a route which seemingly caused a deviation of approximately 350 miles.

The Canary Islands long before had been discovered by the Phoenicians, and it was known that favorable ocean currents moved westerly from the bulge of Africa towards the north tip of South America and the Caribbean Islands. And since the Gulf Stream caused a return flow of ocean currents in the direction of the Azores, it is hardly surprising that the return voyage of Columbus took just that route in returning via a route which ended his Atlantic crossing on the coast of Portugal. That such a voyage could have taken place over the indicated route without the benefit of a great amount of information and prior experience really doesn't seem likely.

For more than 4,000 years prior to the voyage of Columbus, mankind had been slowly, but persistently, advancing from the Stone Age to a way of life utilizing metal tools. As might be expected, those ores which were abundant and easiest to smelt, such as copper and gold, first attracted attention; then it was found that an alloy of copper and tin would produce a hard bronze tool which had many uses which stone tools were unable to satisfy. Once it was realized that metals could be alloyed and blended to advantage, the art of alchemy really began to develop roots.

During the long quest to develop metals, various deposits of iron ore were available, distributed in substantial quantities at numerous places on the earth's surface. Pure iron ore was difficult to produce since the melting point at which it becomes fusible is 1539°C. (2802°F.) Further, since pure iron did not produce a tool equal in hardness to bronze, the search for a suitable alloy and a process of creating usable tools cheaply was very slow to come about. Undoubtedly, iron alloys were created from time to time over many centuries, but any processes so discovered were usually forgotten before they became established. At any rate, by approximately 1,000 B.C. it was found that the addition of 4.3% of carbon would reduce the melting point of pure iron to 1130°C. (2066°F.) and that the alloy so derived would produce hard steel. Once the foregoing breakthrough was mastered, the age of steel was ushered in.

During the foregoing time frame, valuable ores containing metals were almost always secured from high-grade surface outcroppings which could be had without the necessity of underground mining or deep excavations. Surface deposits often played out rather quickly and, since the transportation of heavy ore across land routes where the best roads were simply trails was slow, risky and expensive, the merchant marines of the world took to the high seas in search of ores which might be located in distant lands. The necessity and the pressure for seeking valuable ores was substantially increased when it was realized that the process of alloying metals required the bringing together of ores from various lands. A particular country might have been blessed with ample deposits of, let us say, copper, but to secure the tin to create bronze would require shipments from far-distant Britain. Thus, the various countries of the Mediterranean were pressured more and more to sail to distant lands in search of valuable ores and, hopefully, pre-smelted metals such as copper, silver and gold.

Since ocean craft which occasionally may have reached New World shores prior to Columbus were not embarked upon colonization, we should reflect upon the implements which some of them carried. A successful journey seeking precious ores in remote areas of the world would mandate that the ship's crew be skilled in the use of metal tools and the techniques necessary to extract ore from its earth-bound confines. It was of little use to discover rich outcroppings of ore if the means of extraction were absent. Accordingly, each ship would have carried a variety of metal tools useful for working rock and forest products: sledge hammers, pry bars (crowbars), rasps and coarse files, hammers of various shapes and sizes, picks, wood-cutting axes, cross-cut saws, shovels, grubbing hoes, chisels, and numerous pointed tools of various sizes and shapes. As a matter of fact, almost every ship would have carried an assortment of the foregoing tools for making repairs and for general use irrespective of its mission at a given time.

We can also conclude that a small forge would have been a convenient item on any properly equipped ship.

If a ship's captain were to have made available an assortment of about two dozen good steel tools, a supervised force of workmen could have produced the amazing group of structures at "new" Chich'en Itzá. A knowledgeable estimate suggests that three or four crowbars or similar tools made from steel rods, possibly three or four cross-cut saws, perhaps three straight or curved steel rasps ordinarily used for ship construction or repairs, several axes, a few hammers and sledges, several shovels, and a dozen chisels would have been sufficient to advance stone-working and construction techniques to the level of that which we observe at "new" Chich'en Itzá. Any well-stocked ship of those times could have made available an adequate supply of steel tools without seriously impairing its own requirements.

Those who have dug into the ruins at Chich'en Itzá and elsewhere have been puzzled by the conspicuous absence of evidence of stone-working tools, whether of stone or metal. Scattered pieces or accumulations of broken stone tools made of obsidian, flint or hard limestone haven't been found at "new" Chich'en Itzá, a circumstance which suggests that metal tools could have been used. However, the possibility of ever finding direct evidence of metal tool remnants is extremely remote.

A metal stone-working tool would have been an object highly prized by any Maya workman; in fact, to the Maya of those times a metal tool literally would have been more precious than gold. We can be sure that metal tools would have been closely guarded and precautions taken to prevent their theft or diversion into activities not authorized by those in charge of construction. Broken or worn tools would have been utilized as long as possible, and when the point was reached where a tool no longer served its intended purpose, it would have been converted to some different use so that the precious metal would continue to serve a utilitarian purpose. As an aside, we are told that when Captain Cook explored some of the Pacific Islands during the 1700s, the natives considered a simple nail to be one of the most-prized possessions which could be acquired.

If by sheer accident a metal object might have escaped the grasp of eager users, the humid tropical climate soon would have caused a complete deterioration of its various metal components which were exposed to the elements, such as copper, tin and iron — the metals from which stone-working tools would have been produced.

Archaeologists have heretofore recognized the Mexican influence in the architecture found during the end of the Late Classic era at the Puuc Hills sites, to which they have attached a date of approximately 900 A.D. On the other hand, their calculations applicable to Toltec-Maya construction at "new" Chich'en Itza' suggest an occupancy period of between 1100-1200 A.D. Certain similarities in architectural designs and construction techniques suggest that a void of approximately 200 years without evidence of any significant construction activities might not be realistic; rather, it would appear that construction at "new" Chich'en Itza' commenced soon after construction in the Puuc area, thereby indicating that the time frame assigned to the Late Classic era ought to be advanced to 1000 or 1100 A.D., or alternatively, construction at "new" Chich'en Itza' might have occurred at an earlier date.

It has been with extreme reluctance that I have concluded that the Toltec-Maya built "new" Chich'en Itza' with the assistance of a limited supply of basic steel tools. In arriving at this decision, I am not un mindful that I might have inadvertently fanned the embers of the legend of the "Plumed Serpent" and of the "white, bearded personage." Legends constitute the historical fabric of many ancient peoples, and the stories handed down over hundreds of years become twisted, glorified, and often magnified with very little or no real evidence to support them. On the other hand, to a trial lawyer, hearsay evidence, while generally inadmissible to prove a fact, sometimes furnishes assistance in securing direct evidence. Admittedly, since we have no direct proof of contacts between the Western Hemisphere and other parts of the world prior to Columbus, the foregoing discussion has entered the area of what we term circumstantial evidence, evidence of a type which in the normal course of events and from human experience and logic suggests that a conclusion might be true.

If my analysis and logic supports an argument that the Toltec-

Maya somehow acquired basic steel tools sometime around 1000 A.D., or even before, whether from a shipwreck or from a ship carrying "bearded white personages," we certainly ought to take a somewhat less-skeptical attitude towards the gist of the legend which permeates the folklore of Mesoamerica. There is no point in arguing whether isolated contacts before Columbus were of Asiatic origin, or whether a ship guided by a Viking or some other European or North African might have sailed the waters of the Gulf of Mexico and the Caribbean. That such individuals might have landed on the shores of the Yucatan Peninsula before Columbus is further supported by a profile found on the wall of the North Temple of the Ball Court, sometimes referred to as the Temple of the Bearded Man. There, carved in stone and prominently featured with the effigy of Kukulcan, the "Plumed Serpent," is the precise image of a bearded person for all to see. The inhabitants of Mesoamerica did not grow beards. While there may be a question as to whether the man in the profile might be a Viking, a Celt, an Irishman, a Mediterranean "merchant prince," or some other mariner from an undisclosed land having occasion to be on the high seas, it certainly cannot be denied that his features are neither Maya nor Toltec.

The
Bearded
Man

It is not the purpose of this work to become involved in the controversy over whether Columbus "discovered" America or to discredit the accomplishments of that great explorer. In my opinion, he certainly earned and is entitled to the recognition which has been bestowed upon him. My only point is simply that during the span of many centuries we cannot completely discount the possibility of occasional transpacific or transatlantic contacts with inhabitants of the Western Hemisphere. Actually, I consider the Columbus'-discovery argument to be laid to rest; unfortunately, for too long it has been disruptive of objective research and analysis.

There can be no real comparison between the Maya and their Mesoamerican neighbors when we analyze their achievements in the fields of astronomy, mathematics, calendrical reckonings, sculpture, architecture and stone-working techniques. Considered in the context of the relatively short time interval involved, and focused heavily in the Yucatan Peninsula and adjacent mountain areas, the rapid advance of that civilization must be considered one of the greatest cultural achievements in the history of mankind. Some of the reasons for their amazing exploits have been explained in this book; others defy explanation and leave us wondering.

Except for those arts, sciences, skills and knowledge inherited from the Olmecs, it would seem that the Maya literally raised themselves by their bootstraps on the Yucatan Peninsula and the adjacent rugged mountains of Mesoamerica. In such severe surroundings and in an environment where basic survival must have been a constant challenge, the question logically arises as to what portion of their cultural advancements should be credited to them and what portion might have been acquired from neighboring areas or from other contacts. The inquiry is further complicated by the fact that by the time of the arrival of the Spaniards almost every vestige of their glorious civilization had been abandoned to the jungle and forgotten. It is simply incomprehensible that the legends and folklore which would normally survive such great accomplishments should vanish and fail to be perpetuated.

The Maya had the stone which provided the means whereby

evidence of their Golden Age could be preserved, but other peoples on earth seldom have been so fortunate. We can only laboriously try to put the pieces together and ponder what really took place. When we consider all of the circumstances and problems confronting the artisans and craftsmen who challenged that vast jungle wilderness, we stand amazed, irrespective of whether the great structures were in part influenced by foreign contacts or whether they were entirely indigenous to the Maya. Without by any means demeaning the other great Maya ruins, those of the Puuc Hills (Uxmal, Kab'ah, Sayil and Labná) and Chich'en Itzá, considered together, deserve to be classified as Wonders of the World.

Located on an isolated mound at the end of a jungle trail approximately a mile from the Grand Palace at Sayil, this partially restored building was probably one of the last Late Classic structures ever built.

THE COLLAPSE

It is in the nature of things that civilizations come and go, their demises being attributed to various causes. Archaeologists tell us that by 950 A.D. the major ceremonial centers and most adjacent smaller sites were abandoned, one after another, in a relatively short period of time. The awaiting jungle returned and quietly smothered the evidence of man's presence in its entangling grasp. History teaches us that other civilizations fell, either gradually or suddenly, by reason of devastating wars, changing trade routes, over-population and agricultural failures, and other causes.

The collapse of the Maya has been ascribed to various possible causes: earthquakes, climatic changes, a revolt of the masses against their rulers, disease, agricultural collapse, invasions, and other events. In analyzing the Maya situation, we must keep in mind the fact that their civilization was a Stone Age culture which received its food supply from farming, hunting, fishing (along the rivers and seacoast), and a few other specialized pursuits. It is also to be noted that the collapse of Maya civilization at all inland areas where we find the five major ceremonial centers, as well as at other inland locations, dictates that we search for common denominators.

It is not unknown for civilizations to wither and disappear due to effects of long-range climatic changes, such as have occurred in the Middle East during the course of its turbulent history. But generally, particularly where there has been a population evacuation from a large geographical area due to a severe drouth or similar event, the people have regrouped and returned.

If we accept the fact, as we must, that nearly all of the inland area we have been discussing always had a marginal life-support system, that factor must be viewed in the light of the reasons advanced in this text which account for the great amount of building during Late Classic times. Taking our analysis one step farther, we must ask ourselves whether those same conditions which created the greatness of the Maya might also have contained within themselves limitations which contributed in equal or greater measure to the demise of that civilization.

(a) *A Mobile Population*

The increased level of building construction at the five major ceremonial centers and numerous other smaller sites of the inland Maya country during the Late Classic era would support an assessment that such activities would have drawn greater numbers of people into the area than had existed at those locations at any earlier date. Whether there was a natural population increase in both lowland and highland areas or whether there was primarily a shift of seacoast and highland populations to inland lowland centers might be debatable, but both conditions probably occurred.

The construction of ceremonial centers, albeit with a work force much smaller than heretofore believed necessary, would have required a back-up population of adequate size to furnish food and general supplies. We should also expect that a reasonable amount of trade would have developed with other Maya settlements and such distant population centers as Teotihuacán (near present-day Mexico City). The magnificence of the structures being built would not have been a secret in any part of Mesoamerica.

Various archaeologists have excavated at different locations, and their findings indicate that numerous inland settlements were occupied somewhat permanently or from time to time over many years, but the Late Classic period generally produced greater showings of the presence of larger numbers of people at most sites. We know that Palenque, Tikal and Chich'en Itz'a contained settlements which probably spanned many years, but many of the other inland sites have produced but very few burial caches having meager effects. Further, the important method of establishing dates for human habitation by excavating and examining potsherds, while helpful, has not furnished adequate proof of large population concentrations at many locations.

It is necessary at this point to delve deeper into the mineral resources available to the Maya and to expand upon their possible uses. It was previously noted that modern Portland cement is made from a combination of ingredients consisting primarily of calcium carbonate, silica, alumina and iron, but that the Maya of the Yucatan Peninsula made a reasonably good lime cement by burning nearly pure calcium carbonate so as to recover calcium oxide (CaO). On the other hand, the trachyte deposit found at Cop'an was formed from volcanic pozzolan and clay-type materials, thereby creating a permanent brick-like substance which hardened upon exposure to the elements. Thus, depending upon the availablity of minerals having cementitious qualities, the Maya utilized both organic (limestone) and inorganic (alumina, silica and iron) materials.

Of interest to our discussion, Portland cement combines the cementitious qualities of both organic and inorganic minerals, as illustrated in the following analysis of a representative sample of Portland cement.

Portland Cement Sample

CaO	(burned limestone)....... 64%	}	of organic origin
Al_2O_3	(alumina) 5%		
SiO_2	(silica) 22%	}	of inorganic origin
Fe_2O_3	(iron)................. 3%		
Other ingredients (including gypsum) 6%			
	100%		

By way of comparison, the sample of lime cement taken from the structure at Sayil, which was previously referred to and which is reproduced again below, indicates that the cement produced at most inland Peninsula sites contained very little inorganic mineral content.

Analysis of Puuc Hills Sample

CaO	(burned limestone) 51.45%	}	of organic origin
	Loss on ignition (CO_2) . 43.04%		
Al_2O_3	(alumina)........... 0.08%		
SiO_2	(silica) 3.20%	}	of inorganic origin
Fe_2O_3	(iron) 0.85%		
Other	ingredients 1.38%		
	100.00%		

The foregoing comparisons are relevant to this portion of our discussion because the very small amounts of alumina and silica tell us that the Maya in much of the Yucatan Peninsula had very little or no clay available for their use.

Cement plants producing Portland cement usually find it necessary to secure their four main ingredients from three or four separate sources. On occasion, however, nature has placed in a single deposit nearly all of the four necessary cement-making ingredients in almost the exact percentages necessary to produce Portland cement. That material has been classified as "cement rock," and by definition it is called an argillaceous (clayey or "dirty") limestone. At the present time there are approximately a dozen cement plants in the United States which use cement rock, being located primarily in the Lehigh Valley of Pennsylvania and in the Rocky Mountain states.

When the American West was first settled, limestone kilns — the remains of which sometimes still exist — burned limestone and produced lime cement (CaO) by utilizing the same procedures followed by the Maya. Even as late as the 1930s, I recall that it was the practice of small contractors and farmers to throw two or three shovels full of good country dirt into each batch of concrete which was being mixed so as to add clay to the mixture. Whether that additive made the final concrete mix stronger might be debatable; in any event, the wet concrete mixture was thereby made easier to trowel to a smooth finish, and it appeared to bind together better.

Many writers have commented that Maya aguadas (open storage lakes) were clay lined to retain waters which were abundant during the wet season, but it is highly doubtful that the water-retention material contained much alumina or silica, rather, the term must be applied to that very general definition sometimes attributed to clay as being minute particles of substances of less than four micrometers in size, without regard to the nature of their origin.

Clay minerals of the type important to this discussion are essentially hydrous aluminum silicates composed of non-metallic, inorganic materials (i.e., Al_2O_3 (alumina) plus SiO_2 (silica) plus H_2O (water) = clay).

Good, productive farmlands are highly dependent upon clay compounds to break down and release both organic and inorganic nutrients, and to retain water, necessary for the growth of plant life. Also, the clay-mineral composition of soils greatly affects their ability to be tilled and to be treated with fertilizers. Agronomists are well aware of the critical role played by clay in agricultural production; they likewise know that crops do poorly in limestone soils of the type found in most of the inland Yucatan Peninsula — another reason explaining the poverty of the earth and its inability to produce crops for any extended length of time.

The lack of clay minerals had another significant impact upon Maya life across the inland Peninsula in that the ingredients for making brick and pottery were mostly absent. Archaeologists and others who have studied Maya life in the inland Peninsula area are nearly unanimous in believing that active trading was a way of life, yet relatively little attention has been focused upon the extent of trade with other Maya in the highlands and in lowland coastal and river valleys in order to secure pottery — perhaps because digs have revealed only limited amounts of pottery objects at many locations.

Ceramic items which may have been produced at most inland Peninsula locations would have been very crude and cold-molded (not fired) due to the near absence of alumina and the abundance of calcium carbonates. The refractoriness of clay increases in proportion to the amount of alumina found in the clay — kaolin, a good fireclay, is in the range of 38% Al_2O_3 — and decreases when impurities such as calcium carbonate ($CaCO_3$) are present.

It is understandable that a seminomadic people living from the earth primarily by hunting and gathering would have had less need for pottery vessels and utensils due to the type of food available and the manner of its preparation and because of the requirement of instant mobility in the search for sustenance. Small pottery utensils which could have been easily carried — and which constitute most of the evidence available at this time — are indications of mobile groups of hunters and gatherers who may have brought their pottery objects and other necessities from some other more-permanent location.

On the other hand, a settled urban community would have required the importation of substantial quantities of pottery vessels because the unavailability of clay would have prevented any local cottage industry from being pursued. At Palenque, where the nearby mountains and the Usumacinta River valley would be expected to furnish deposits of clay for making pottery and ceramics, the limited finds of potsherds suggests that there was relatively little local production of pottery.

One disturbing feature common to excavations at many sites has been the failure to discover substantial numbers of pottery vessels of sizes approximating five gallons or larger, since large storage containers would have been needed where people congregated in order to store water, maize, salt, and many other essentials of urban life. A fairly large deposit of broken pottery vessels, including some which would have held more than five gallons of water, was discovered in a Puuc Hills cave which led down to an underground water source; however, the source of clay from which they were made apparently has not been determined, and it is probable that they were imported into the area. The existence and location of available clay deposits on the Yucatan Peninsula in Late Classic times, as well as the location and extent of related pottery and ceramic-manufacturing activities, are intriguing subjects which require further investigation and study.

The limited number of finds of pottery containers of large sizes is another indication that the Late Classic Maya were very mobile and that many of their ceremonial centers may have been occupied seasonally, or even for shorter intervals, as groups of people moved from place to place across that difficult and uncompromising land in search of food and water.

The relative scarcity of potsherds, burial caches and similar evidence of the debris of long-term human habitation fails to provide supporting proof necessary to establish the existence of large cities in the inland area. Even in those locations where archaeologists believe that very small mounds or indications of perishable structures seemingly furnish proof of human occupation, a single family unit could have had a living area and several out-buildings devoted to related uses, or even an additional residence, each occupied during different seasons, all of which could be erroneously attributed to abodes of several families.

From all available evidence, it must be concluded that the number of inhabitants at many inland sites during Late Classic times would not have been great, and such larger population concentrations as there may have been probably existed at some sites for only short periods of time. Except during periods of large construction activities, most settlements would have supported populations of not more than

2,000 people. Cop'an, Palenque and Uxmal probably never had in excess of 5,000 people living within a radius of three miles from their respective ceremonial centers, and the maximum populations of Tikal or Chich'en Itz'a within the same distance from their respective ceremonial centers never would have exceeded 10,000 people. I do not believe the entire Yucatan Peninsula area which is now within the borders of Mexico and Guatemala contained more than 1,000,000 people at any time during the Late Classic era. It is entirely possible, however, that the total population of the Peninsula would have been considerably larger if we include the area encompassed within present-day Belize.

From all indications at our disposal at the present time, it would appear that the Late Classic era was characterized by a very mobile population, both because of the side effects of construction activities and because of the inability of different settlements at various times to sustain their inhabitants due to the factors we have previously discussed. The sudden loss of a domestic water supply, or a drouth which wiped out an agricultural crop, would have forced sudden moves upon communities. Migrating groups of starving and thirsty people intent upon survival would have posed a threat to neighboring communities, and it may have been a few experiences of that type which forced Becan to construct a large, open-ditch fortification around its community center.

The development of large, imposing ceremonial centers would have tended to spawn an elite, and possibly war-like, element with leanings toward pomp and ceremony, elaborate costumes, social status, and all of the trappings associated with the grandeur of their ceremonial centers and the power which naturally flows into the hands of those who would lead. The refinement of such possibilities and their effect on the religious, political and social life of the Maya is a subject best left to the appropriate specialists.

It is easy to let one's imagination run wild and envision great numbers of people living in the larger ceremonial centers during Late Classic times, particularly in view of the long-held erroneous belief that hordes of workmen were required to build them. But when we look at

A portion of the reconstructed Bonampak murals depicting an elaborate ceremony featuring prisoners taken in battle for sacrificial purposes. Bonampak was a small Late Classic Maya site located on a tributary of the Usumacinta River approximately 80 miles southeast of Palenque.

the situation realistically, knowing that the job could have been done by a limited number of workmen over a relatively short period of time and that conditions for supporting large numbers of people were lacking at many of the large inland centers, a more-sober estimate of population concentration is in order.

A most convincing argument advanced in support of conservative population estimates is that the physical size of the larger — and even many smaller — inland ceremonial centers did not necessarily bear a direct relationship to the actual size of the populations they served. Once it is realized that the size of each of the five major ceremonial centers was dependent upon, and ultimately limited by, the size and extent of available bedded-stone deposits, it then becomes necessary to adopt a different criteria for making population estimates. It is this last-stated proposition which tips the scales of belief in favor of those archaeologists who have long contended that the five large ceremonial centers were never really cities in the true sense of the word.

(b) *Seeds of its Own Destruction*

Theorists attempting to analyze the collapse of Maya civilization almost uniformly refer to the failure of the various ceremonial centers to continue the erection of commemorative stelae. Stelae constituted one of the major methods whereby sculpture, glyphs and dates were preserved, and the cessation of that practice understandably was a traumatic archaeological event since the dated history of the Maya abruptly ended.

Did the last stelae, which bears a date the equivalent of 909 A.D., coincide exactly with the termination of all construction at the end of the Late Classic era, or did construction continue beyond that date? No hard and fast answer can be furnished but, subject to a few qualifications which a better understanding of stelae construction will reveal, Late Classic construction probably continued for a reasonable time thereafter — possibly until 950 A.D.

When the Maya quarried a large slab of stone of uniform consistency and with at least one reasonably smooth face, an attempt was often made to use it as a stela, thus recording dates, rulers, gods, scenes and glyphs. Once more, the type and availability of building materials at the various ceremonial centers dictated the use of stelae. A good stela stone also had to be two or more feet wide and, preferably, taller than a man; in fact, the taller the better. But the availability of suitable stones meeting those specifications was another matter. Acceptable stelae stones, as well as lintel stones of sufficient length and proper width to span room openings, were in short supply everywhere. Their availability was subject to the conditions which existed when the stone deposits were created by nature.

A stone slab which contained even a hairline cross-fracture could not be used for the simple reason that it would break from pounding, chipping or similar shocks and vibrations. It is in the nature of most bedded-stone deposits that perfect specimens of stones having lengths of, say, six to ten feet have also been packaged by nature with proportionate thicknesses of depth and width, and it was this circumstance which provided large rectangular stelae slabs in the volcanic trachyte deposit at Cop'an and the thick upper layers of the limestone deposits at Tikal. The corresponding layers in the Puuc deposits and at Chich'en Itz'a appear to have been less susceptible to producing stelae stones due to a greater prevalence of cross-fractured or coarse-grained slabs, or both. At Palenque, the hard, brittle nature of the limestone produced a very limited number of poor-quality stelae slabs, thus forcing its artisans to create sculpture, dates and glyphs through the medium of plaster placed on the walls of their structures. Undoubtedly, Cop'an and Tikal had by far the best stelae- producing stone deposits.

We have previously mentioned that it was necessary to remove the thick caprock when quarrying was initiated at some Peninsula sites in order to reach the first bedded layer from which most stelae were probably made. As William R. Coe pointed out with respect to the Tikal stelae, and as I have previously commented, the granular composition of that upper limestone layer used to produce the earlier stelae was not as fine grained and consistent as that which was found in other layers of that and other Peninsula deposits. However, the Maya were required to somehow use or dispose of those large slabs before they could get to the better layers underneath, and so we find that stelae were constructed at Tikal over a period of roughly 250 years pre-dating Late Classic times.

We must also conclude that the removal of the thick, topmost bedded layer from the various deposits in order to reach better-quality building stone layers caused a fairly early elimination of available stelae slabs, unless of course — and this seems improbable — they were set aside for use as much as a hundred years or more in the future. Consequently, it would be reasonable to assume that the erection of stelae usually ceased at some time prior to the termination of all construction activities at any given ceremonial center.

If the reader had been following this discourse carefully, a question might logically arise concerning the reason why no other writers have adopted the premise that the most elaborate ceremonial centers were constructed of deposits of bedded building stone consisting of several layers. A corollary matter to ponder would suggest that the most convincing evidence would be to produce photographs of stone deposits of the type being discussed.

To the experienced quarrier who has found the right trail to follow the evidence is everywhere: the unusual appearance of, and the variations among, the building stone faces; the shape of the facing stones which were broken and trimmed after being quarried; the absence of quarry "holes in the ground"; the voluminous amount of waste rubble stone produced; and other telltale showings. But the present existence of a good, undisturbed bedded-stone deposit of the type under discussion cannot, and probably will not, be found. The explanation has involved a great amount of travel, research and personal study.

In the general vicinity of the ceremonial centers at Chich'en Itz'a, Uxmal, Kab'ah, Sayil and Tikal there can be found numerous small secondary structures, with an occasional small pyramid alongside, placed upon satellite mounds. The Maya were not content to utilize all available stone where the ceremonial centers were located; they extended their search into the surrounding countryside and quarried and utilized every mound of bedded stone, howbeit ever so small or isolated.

The usual method of working small, isolated deposits was that of quarrying and setting aside all usable building stone, dumping the waste rubble stone over the edge of the mound, and then constructing a single building on the leveled quarry floor. The method adopted (except that pyramids were less often found at smaller sites) was simply a modified variation of that which was followed at the larger centers. Since the structure on each mound completely utilized all of the bedded-stone deposit, a good estimate can be formed as to the size and appearance of the original stone deposit from examining the stone in the building.

My extended search, though somewhat more limited than I might have desired, and always hampered by the ever present jungle, failed to reveal a single mound or other area with an existing deposit of layered stone. Quite frankly, the Maya got there first. It can be assum-

The Mirador at Sayil, like numerous other ruins in the Yucatan Peninsula, occupies a single mound. The Maya quarried stone and built on-site everywhere.

ed that the discovery basic to much of the content of this book would have been made many years ago had such obvious evidence been present.

One can examine recently constructed road cuts through the Puuc Hills, to the south and east of Merida, and south of Tikal, and find little evidence suggesting the presence of bedded-stone deposits of the type which were available to the Maya. Small, broken, layered formations of limestone in highway cuts near Kab'ah and Chich'en Itz'a are of some help, however, with showings of soft interstitial material similar to that which separated the layers of the better stone deposits that once existed.

One of the better places to look for indications of bedded stone is the large cenote at Chich'en Itz'a. Around the upper reaches of the

Evidence of bedded-stone layers can be seen around the west side of the cenote at Chich'en Itz'a.

cenote there can be observed layered stone strata in several places which, though badly fractured and poorly bedded, suggest the appearance of the much better deposit found by the Maya some 1,000 feet farther south.

If the advocates of the proposition that the Yucatan Peninsula contained inexhaustible supplies of easily cut building stone had ever extended their thinking to a logical conclusion, it would be expected that such beautiful and desirable stone would be widely used today on private, commercial and public buildings, particularly in the cities and resort complexes around the Peninsula. In an age of metal hand tools, air drills, blasting substances, earth-moving equipment and diamond cutting saws, stone of the quality available to the Maya at Chich'en Itz'a, Uxmal and Tikal would be highly prized for its workability and as a beautiful decorative or structural component of almost any type of

A heavy mass of caprock overlays several strata of bedded stone on the east side of the cenote at Chichén Itzá. The bedded layers are of relatively poor quality.

building. Instead, we find that the applications which do exist (such as the air terminal in Merida) utilize stone slabs which have been subjected to sawing, splitting and shaping processes requiring the use of machine tools. Most of the stone so used has been sorted and processed in conjunction with aggregates operations (i.e., sand-, gravel- and ballast-type materials) in the vicinity of Merida and a few other cities of the Peninsula. Because of the efforts and costs involved, the use of machine-made stone has been limited. It should also be noted that the above-mentioned stone is secured mostly from solid deposits; in those rare instances where bedding planes are encountered, the stone surfaces are usually very rough.

The Maya left very little bedded stone for those who followed in their paths.

There was a fairly large deposit of bedded limestone at Merida when the Spaniards founded the city in 1542. Bishop Diego de Landa, writing of the surrounding Yucatan area, observed that at Merida (called Tihoo by the Maya) a "large and beautiful mound" of stone was being systematically quarried nearby.

When John L. Stephens wrote *"Incidents of Travel in Yucatan"* during the 1840s, he was given to understand that the Plaza Major at Merida was located on the spot where there once existed a mound of stone, and that just to the east of it was another mound. In his book he passes along information that the mounds were so large that the stones were used by the Spaniards to build all the edifices in the city. He quotes from a Spanish chronicler at the time of the Conquest who stated, as to the mounds referred to above, that one interfered with the city layout and that another had ancient buildings on it. The fact that dimension stone could be secured for building a cathedral was undoubtedly a consideration in establishing Merida at its present location.

The Spaniards made it a practice of building a cathedral as soon as possible after establishing any New World colony, primarily for the purpose of controlling the native population by the device of directing their religious practices and beliefs. But they brought their Christian God, and they made Him the God of the Maya and established Him in cathedrals across the land, even though the Maya stubbornly retained many of their ancient religious beliefs and practices.

Once again, the Maya were conscripted for the purpose of constructing temples for a different god who would take the place of those who had served them throughout the ages. And, where convenient, usable stone in their ancient ruins was used to build cathedrals where the new god could be properly worshipped.

One can visit the cathedrals and some of the other old buildings in the center of Merida and observe the blocks of stone quarried from that large mound which existed when the Spaniards arrived. Revealing the same range of depth found in the bedded layers of other Peninsula deposits — 11, 14, 15, 16, 19 and 22 inches — the availability of metal

The Cathedral at Merida.

tools at that time enabled the masons to create cube-shaped blocks having right-angled corners on at least one end of each block. As a result, the blocks were very valuable in establishing the vertical corner columns of those major structures. The stones can be examined today, and the exterior walls between the stone corner columns reveal a mixture of broken limestone rock embedded in concrete.

The limestone layers in the deposit at Merida were coarse grained and they lacked the uniform consistency of the stone layers found at Chich'en Itz'a and Uxmal. An examination clearly shows the presence of small sea shells and other discrete objects embedded randomly within each stone block. Because of this feature, the Maya were unable to effect controlled breaks by their available techniques without shattering the stone into undersirable shapes, and so the deposit remained unused until more sophisticated metal tools became available, thus enabling the blocks of stone to be stacked one-upon-the-other in a cathedral — an enlargement upon the "old" method of stone laying which was followed prior to the Late Classic era.

As the city of Merida began to grow in colonial times, it is reasonable to believe that its developers often wished that the mound of stone was much larger or that they could find another nearby mound of bedded stone — which, obviously, was not available.

Stephens traveled extensively in the area around and between Uxmal and Merida, as well as to the east of Merida. He repeatedly stressed his belief that the native Maya of his time were descendants of those who built the ruins he observed. Also, he was acutely conscious of the scarcity of drinking water for his horses and the members of his traveling party. Among other interesting observations was his reference to numerous ramon trees found in close proximity to many of the ruins he visited.

Noteworthy among his observations was that an examination of more than 40 ruins in the northern Yucatan revealed that all of them, including even the smaller ones consisting of a single building or two, were always found on mounds. Repeated references to ruins on mounds can be found throughout his book.

Although the larger ceremonial centers required the construction efforts of what we would consider to be a modest-sized crew of workmen, the smaller outlying mounds scattered around the Peninsula could have been quarried and a building placed thereon in as little as a year's time by as few as two to six workmen. Since drinking water was in such short supply at most places, we can conclude that those who quarried and built one or two structures on a single, isolated mound often did so without establishing a permanent residence nearby. All this must lead us to the conclusion that, whether the individual worked alone or as a member of a construction crew, his religious requirements were peculiarly and completely satisfied by erecting a temple to his gods. In addition, the need for self-expression was satisfied in the excellent quality of his workmanship.

If there is any merit to the argument which has been advanced that the Maya "collapse" involved a revolt of downtrodden masses against harsh rulers, it would have probably occurred in a somewhat different manner than has been suggested. Quite understandably, if the construction of ceremonial centers required workers conscripted from established settlements near the seacoast or in river valleys in, say, what is now Belize, and taken to an inland construction site for a tour of duty under harsh and oppressive living conditions, the sharp contrast might have outweighed the fervor of a religious crusade.

(c) *Technology vs. Finite Resources*

The Maya have provided us with the best possible example of the time-worn cliché, for they literally didn't leave a stone unturned. With diligence and tenacity, they sought out and quarried every deposit of good bedded stone that could be found; in short, they high-graded their most valuable resource to the point of extinction. Just like the ore miners of the western United States, their mineral resources played out. The conclusion is inescapable: *The various projects completely quarried and exhausted their deposits of bedded building stone.*

The explosion of building activity in Late Classic times could have been partly attributable to competition among the rulers of the various large ceremonial centers, each trying to outdo the other. Such competition would have hastened the utilization and exhaustion of the inferior and easily gathered surface caprock at logical population sites such as Cobá and Mayapán, as well as the best bedded-stone deposits wherever found.

We are now in a good position to assess the effect that the loss of their stone sources had upon the collapse of Maya civilization. Admittedly, attributing a major cause of the decline to the exhaustion of their only source of building material inserts a new and different element into a subject which for too long has been shrouded in mystery; in fact, the situation has evolved to the point where acknowledging the impossibility of solving the mysteries surrounding the collapse of the Maya has assumed as much priority as attempting to search for their solutions. Mysteries provide the stuff from which novels and entertaining trips of the imagination are made; one must always ponder the propriety of entering their sacred domain.

Devastating earthquakes have been suggested as a cause of the Maya collapse — but the lowland Yucatan Peninsula has always been immune from the instability of the earthquake-prone highlands, such as the region near present-day Guatemala City; a peasantry rising in revolt against harsh rulers has been advanced — but the volume of quarrying and construction evidenced on small, individual mounds, plus the fact that the number of workmen necessary to construct the large ceremonial centers was not great, all tend to downplay that possibility as a causative factor; invasions by foreigners has been suggested, but the general poverty of the area would make one wonder why any outsiders would have coveted the inland Maya country — actually, the reverse would appear to be every bit as logical; epidemics and diseases, while they cannot be completely discounted, would have run their course, and it would be expected that the population would have restored its numbers in due time and re-established once-deserted settlements.

The one overriding premise which has been advanced in this book is that the inland Yucatan Peninsula, in particular, always presented the problem of providing sufficient food and water for any sizable permanent population, and, as pointed out, slight variations in climatic conditions could have caused sudden movements of considerable numbers of people during short periods of time. But to attribute the collapse of a civilization and the abandonment of a large region to that cause alone lacks several necessary elements of finality. This assessment is further supported by recent studies which tend to establish that climatic conditions which existed before, during and after the Late Classic era did not substantially change. On the other hand, Late Classic population pressure reduced both the quantity and quality of the food supply by reducing the amount of wild game and contributing to a declining supply of agricultural foods. According to some recent studies of skeletal remains, the height of the average Maya became four to six inches shorter, a condition attributed to limited supplies of food having steadily declining nutritional value.

The conditions which appear to have been common to much of the Maya world would appear to have been (a) poor and unproductive jungle land, coupled with a shortage of rainfall when most needed; (b) a common all-pervading religion; and (c) limestone caprock or bedded-stone deposits scattered at random across the countryside, the best of which were completely utilized. It was this last occurrence which this writer submits to have been the major contributing factor which in-itiated the decline of Maya civilization between 800 and 900 A.D. across the inland Peninsula. It was the catalyst which brought together several latent weaknesses in the Maya economic system which had been gathering strength for some time.

Just as the existence and means of utilizing the unusual bedded-stone deposits was undoubtedly one of the most important reasons for the rise of their civilization, the exhaustion of that raw material resource was a major cause of its demise. The great surge of building activity across the area created excesses which, like the tide, eventually fell back and sought their natural levels. Broadly speaking, this is one example of a civilization having run its course.

When the workmen quarried the last of the bedded-stone deposits at a given site, they often found   and sometimes with little advance warning — that there were no more stelae to be curved and no more majestic buildings and pyramids to be constructed. The quarriers and masons were literally out of work; and since there was no reason for them to remain, they disbanded or moved on to another construction site. In the normal course of events the exhaustion of the stone deposits would have been anticipated in advance, with the result that the departure from any particular ceremonial building site in the absence of drouth or some other unusual adverse condition would have been gradual and uneventful.

We must not lose sight of the fact that stone, in one form or another, constituted very nearly 100% of the building material at all of the ceremonial centers. It was the only permanent building material available to that ancient people, and in their stone-work they have revealed much of the story of their existence. The Maya could not replace their essential building material; and there were no substitutes — not even brick. The Phoenicians went into decline as a great seafaring people when their forests (the cedars of Lebanon) were cut and destroyed; likewise, the Maya were no longer able to continue as the greatest Stone Age builders on earth when their bedded-stone deposits were exhausted.

Nothing in the rituals or beliefs of the religion of the Maya was oriented in the direction of long-term maintenance of their structures. This seems to be further evident from the fact that some buildings were periodically demolished and new structures were placed upon the debris of the old. It is understandable that the Maya erected structures so long as, and on every mound where, they could find bedded limestone.

All excesses of human activity eventually reach the point where they come to a halt and negative reactions set in. That time had come for the Maya when they ran out of their premier building material. It was that event which caused all construction to terminate at site after site, sometimes forcing partially built structures to be abandoned when a stone source unexpectedly played out sooner than anticipated. The momentum of great construction ceased and yielded to the quiet course of history.

It is easy to appreciate the devastating effect of the cessation of building activities when the moving force began to disintegrate and the lifestyle of a given ceremonial complex absorbed such a crippling blow. Not only was the stage set for an out-migration of most of the population attached to the work force, but there was less inducement for the curious to make pilgrimages to a ceremonial center after construction terminated.

The time frame during which the collapse occurred has been tied to dates on the various stelae found at various ceremonial sites, indicating that construction activities terminated in sequence over a period of approximately 150 years. Subject to the qualification that construction at a given site probably extended 50 or as much as 100 years beyond the date of the last stelae, which would have had the effect of advancing the time in terms of years of calendrical reckoning, I would concur that 150 years is not unreasonable. The disturbing problem which presents itself is that of coming up with a realistic assessment of the impact which would have been created over such an extended length of time upon a Stone Age people.

At those ceremonial sites built from the better deposits of bedded stone, the exhaustion of that building material and the cessation of building activities could have caused a sudden and almost complete population exodus if soil and water resources were so marginal that a community could not have established and maintained a permanent base nearby. That condition would have been present at Tikal, Uxmal and other Puuc sites, and to a somewhat lesser extent at Chich'en Itza. Palenque would have been similarly abandoned, but its population would have been absorbed in community settlements along the base of the Chiapas Mountains and in the nearby highland valleys. As for Cop'an, the actual population displacement probably was not great because the craftsmen and artisans could have shifted to another construction site and the local workers and their families would have moved a short distance farther down the river valley and settled in small communities in locations where they exist today.

On the other hand, any Maya settlement, whether located on the inland Peninsula, near the seashore, in a river valley or at a highland location, probably would have experienced insignificant population disruption if there had been available year-round water and reasonably productive crop lands. In this latter category we would expect to find true cities, such as Cob'a, Mayap'an and Dzibilchaltun, as well as settlements around many ceremonial centers where crude pyramid temples and other structures were erected of local caprock and sometimes covered with plaster. The magnitude of population displacement, as well as any possible reduction in the total Maya population, at the end of the Late Classic era would have likely been insignificant in comparison to the great loss of life from battles, famine and imported diseases brought by the Spanish Conquest several hundred years later.

The time had arrived when the proliferating ceremonial centers became so numerous and their competition probably so intense as to thin out the area of influence of each. Coupled with that development, it is only natural that the novelty of the great edifices being constructed gradually wore away. The collapse was manifested most directly in a malaise which descended when construction activities terminated. The resulting void adversely affected the continuance and development of arts and crafts, stunted religious fervor, created serious and drastic social and political rearrangements, and halted scientific and cultural advancement. Its effects permeated the entire lowland area.

With the termination of construction activities at most ceremonial centers, it was not long before the inhabitants gathered their meager effects and retreated to areas in the mountains, river valleys and seacoast locations where farming was better and where they could utilize the sea for trading and fishing. The so-called migration never involved "millions" of people; at most, there may have been a few thousand involved at a given time. With no incentive for the inhabitants to expend any substantial effort in simple maintenance work on their glorious structures, they moved on and their great works became ghost towns.

The Maya ultimately had to face the realization that their days of greatness were numbered and that the accomplishments of their craftsmen would be abandoned to the jungle. The glory of their civilization did not collapse with a bang — it exited quietly and with barely a whimper.

The rise and fall of the Maya during the Late Classic era is one of the most fascinating episodes in history. They developed a technology which made it possible to utilize an unusual, finite resource, and they constructed some of the greatest edifices on earth in a land mostly devoid of any other valuable resource. Their technology enabled them to utilize and ultimately consume the special gift from which the brilliance of their civilization has been measured; in short, their technology outpaced their raw material resources. Similar "overshoot" occurrences have been recorded throughout history, but that of the Maya stands apart because it was a unique Stone Age version.

214

SUPPLEMENT I
ABODES FOR GODS

One of the most striking aspects of Maya life was the abundance of deities available for their worship. Whether found in scriptures, paintings or stone sculptures, the worship of many gods in elaborate religious ceremonies pervaded their lives. Almost every permanent stone structure built by the Maya, whether in appearance a pyramid, palace or temple, was used at least in part for religious purposes.

The facades of structures built of good bedded stone provided ideal locations for the stone images of Maya gods; in other places, where the limitations of available stone did not permit such craftsmanship, they utilized local caprock for their structures and adorned the concrete mass with images composed of plaster and paint.

The Maya had gods for each day of the month and each month of the year. Gods held up the earth, and gods lived in the thirteen compartments of heaven and the nine compartments of the underworld. Many gods were closely related to nature and the forces of nature. Some gods were more important than others, and the flexible Maya religion provided a new god whenever there appeared a function which needed to be performed.

The Rain God Chac appears over 200 times in the Maya codices surviving the destruction of their literature by Bishop de Landa, and Chac masks are widely found in stone carvings and mosaics at many Maya ceremonial sites. Chac was primarily associated with prayers for rain, also portrayed as a symbol of death. Many Maya gods, including the all-encompassing Itzamná (sometimes referred to as the Sun God), expressed this duality of nature, being both benevolent or revengeful as the occasion or conditions dictated.

On the other hand, certain gods were almost always presented as youthful, benevolent or beneficial. The Corn God, Yum Kaax (also sometimes known as Itzamná and Kan), always appeared youthful and wore maize as a headdress. Obviously this god was very important to the Maya since he symbolized the importance of maize in their lives. Kukulcan, generally referred to as Quetzalcóatl, the "Plumed Serpent," was the God of November and was a benevolent god associated with the exchange of gifts. It is believed that Kukulcan was the ruler who rebuilt Chich'en Itzá after the close of the Late Classic era.

It is believed that human sacrifice was not customarily practiced until Post Classic times, although blood letting in sacrificial ceremonies was prevalent during the Late Classic era. In some ceremonial centers the priests believed that the Sun God (Ahau) went to the underworld at night completely devoid of strength and that in order to continue another day's journey they had to furnish him with new blood. Reliable evidence suggests that prisoners were often required to sacrifice blood to satisfy the Sun God.

Space and purpose preclude any attempt to list the many Maya gods. Their diversity can best be stated by acknowledging that numerous gods were always available to provide guidance, protection and companionship in the forbidding and difficult jungle and mountainous lands of Mesoamerica where survival presented an ever present challenge.

•

THE MAYA NUMBERS SYSTEM

PROBLEM:

$$\begin{array}{c}\overline{\quad}\\ \ominus \\ \bullet\bullet\bullet \\ \bullet\end{array} \qquad =?$$

SOLUTION:

Key —

$$\ominus \quad = \quad 0$$

$$\bullet \quad = \quad 1$$

$$\overline{\quad\quad} \quad = \quad 5$$

$$\underset{=}{\bullet\bullet\bullet} \quad = \quad 13$$

Computation —

8,000 (20 x 20 x 20)	X	▬	(5)	=	40,000
400 (20 x 20)	X	⊖	(0)	—	- - -
20	X	▪▪▪	(13)	=	260
units		•	(1)	=	1
					40,261

The Maya kept track of time by numbering days according to a system which was subject to precise calculation. They devised symbols which expressed the basics of the system: zero was usually a shell, and numbers were represented by dots and dashes with each dot equaling one unit and each dash representing five units. Instead of units of ten being used to express the equivalent of a decimal system, the Maya based their system on units of twenty.

The symbols representing the numbers were usually placed one above the other in a vertical column, but the position of each symbol in the column was extremely important because each level which it occupied, starting at the bottom and working upward, operated as a decimal shift so as to give the symbol a different value. Thus, for each location in the column above the first, the symbol was multiplied by 20. In other words, all symbols on the second level were multiplied by 20, those on the third level were multiplied by 400 (i.e., 20 X 20), those on the fourth level were multiplied by 8,000 (i.e., 20 X 20 X 20), and so on. By multiplying the symbol value by the multiple applicable to its location in the vertical column, and then adding the results so arrived at from all of the various symbols, the number of days could be determined as set forth in the illustration on the preceding page.

From the foregoing it was possible to calculate time. A day represented one *kin*, a month of 20 days represented a *uinal*, a numerical year of 360 days was a *tun*, 20 numerical years was a *katun*, and 400 numerical years measured a *baktun*. The Maya calendar commenced with baktun 13, or the equivalent of the year 3113 B.C.

The Maya calendar year (365.2420 days) was more accurate than our Gregorian calendar year (365.2425 days), and it corresponded almost precisely with the solar year (365.2422 days) computed by modern astronomers.

INDEX

Erasmus, Charles J.: 67-68

— F —

farming (see Agriculture): 111, 140,
    195
flint: 14, 29, 128, 184
food: 136, 140, 142
foreign invasions: 116-119, 187, 210
Funerary Crypt (Palenque): 1 (photo),
    109, 115, 151

— G —

geology: 8, 139, 167
ghost towns: 78, 163, 214
glyphs: 114, 200
gods: 215-216
Grand Palace (Sayil): 94 (photo),
    97 (photo), 98 (photo)
Great Plaza (Tikal): 13 (photo),
    15, 21
Great Pyramid, The (Uxmal): 76
    (photo), 80
Guatemala: 1-3, 4 (map)
Guatemala City, Guatemala: 4
    (map), 9
Gulf of Mexico: 4 (map)

H

hardness of limestone: 6, 18, 25
Hieroglyphic Stairway (Copán): 113-
    116, 116 (photo)
"Highlands": 2, 5
honey: 140
Honduras: 1, 4 (map)
houses (huts): 3 (photo)

— I —

Inca: 157, 160-162
    Cusco: 159, 163
    Machu Picchu: 157, 159-160, 160
        (photo), 161-163, 162 (photo)
Inscriptions, Temple of (Palenque):
    1, 108, 109 (photo), 151
iron: 180, 182

Itzamná (Corn God): 215

— J —

jade: 115
jungle: 1-3, 9, 26, 133-142

— K —

KABÁH: 28 (map), 95, 95 (photo),
    96
    Palace of the Masks: 95 (photo)
kilns: 64-65, 65 (sketch), 68
Kohunlich, Mexico: 27, 130
Kukulcan: 166, 170, 186, 216
Kukulcan, Pyramid of (Chichén
    Itzá): 29 (photo), 30, 37, 40-41
    (photo), 42-43

— L —

Labná: 28 (map), 77, 99, 99 (photo)
Lake Petén (Guatemala): 4 (map), 13
Landa, Diego de: 140, 206
Late Classic era (references): 11, 22-
    24, 58, 72, 76, 104-105, 110
    (photo), 113, 115, 124, 133-134,
    142, 146, 148-152, 154, 165,
    167-168, 170-172, 176-177, 185,
    190, 192-193, 197-201, 208-210,
    214
Lhuillier, Alberto Ruz: 109, 119
limestone: 5-7, 33-39, 53-55, 60-62,
    88, 104, 127-129, 141
lintels: 8, 70, 176
"Lowlands": 2
Lubaantun, Belize: 127

— M —

machete: 142
Machu Picchu: 157, 159-160, 160
    (photo), 161-162, 162 (photo), 163
maize: 140, 163
manioc: 140
Mayapán, Mexico: 122, 122 (map),
    124-130
measurement, unit of: 19, 46, 95, 186